☼Hokuriku p64

☼Shanghai p114

ASIA

Sikkim p52 ☼   Hunan p84 ☼

PACIFIC
OCEAN

☼Malaysia p46

☼Seychelles p34

INDIAN
OCEAN

The Kimberley p56 ☼

Ha'apai p88 ☼

AUSTRALIA

Adelaide p126 ☼

Auckland p130 ☼

West Coast p80 ☼

☼Antarctica p14

LONELY PLANET'S

BEST in TRAVEL

2014

THE BEST TRENDS, DESTINATIONS, JOURNEYS & EXPERIENCES FOR THE UPCOMING YEAR

MELBOURNE | OAKLAND | LONDON

INTRODUCTION 6

TOP 10 COUNTRIES 8

BRAZIL 10
ANTARCTICA 14
SCOTLAND 18
SWEDEN 22
MALAWI 26

MEXICO 30
SEYCHELLES 34
BELGIUM 38
MACEDONIA 42
MALAYSIA 46

TOP 10 REGIONS 50

SIKKIM, INDIA 52
THE KIMBERLEY,
  AUSTRALIA 56
YORKSHIRE, UK 60
HOKURIKU, JAPAN 64
TEXAS, USA 68

VICTORIA FALLS,
  ZIMBABWE & ZAMBIA 72
MALLORCA, SPAIN 76
WEST COAST, NEW ZEALAND .. 80
HUNAN, CHINA 84
HA'APAI, TONGA 88

TOP 10 CITIES 92

PARIS, FRANCE 94
TRINIDAD, CUBA 98
CAPE TOWN, SOUTH AFRICA 102
RĪGA, LATVIA 106
ZÜRICH, SWITZERLAND 110

SHANGHAI, CHINA 114
VANCOUVER, CANADA 118
CHICAGO, USA 122
ADELAIDE, AUSTRALIA 126
AUCKLAND, NEW ZEALAND 130

TOP TRAVEL LISTS   134

BEST VALUE DESTINATIONS 136

SPECIAL ANNIVERSARIES 140

BEST FAMILY TRAVEL 144

BEST HONEYMOON DESTINATIONS 148

BEST ADVENTURE TRAVEL 152

BEST BEACHES & SMALL ISLANDS 156

100 YEARS SINCE THE FIRST WORLD WAR 160

BEST BEATLEMANIA 164

TOP SHAKESPEARIAN SITES 168

WHERE TO WIN YOUR OWN WINTER OLYMPICS 172

WHERE TO FEEL LIKE ONE OF THE FAMILY 176

BEST LUXURY BOOT CAMPS 180

SIGHTS TO MAKE YOU FEEL SMALL 184

BEST PLACES TO GET DRESSED FOR SUCCESS 188

HIDDEN FOODIE HIGHLIGHTS 192

BEST CLASSIC CAR RIDES 196

THE CAT'S MEOW 200

INDEX 204

ACKNOWLEDGEMENTS 206

BEST IN TRAVEL PLANNER 2014 208

HERE AT LONELY PLANET OUR FEET CONTINUALLY ITCH. TRAVEL'S IN THE BLOOD OF EVERYONE WHO WORKS HERE.

Holidays are meticulously planned, eagerly anticipated and then, to the agony of those of us stuck at home, replayed to a green-faced audience. *Best in Travel* aims to make sure you're the one with stories to tell rather than the one stuck at home.

This year, like in previous years, we're making suggestions for the cities, countries and regions we think you should consider visiting in 2014. Top picks Paris, Brazil and Sikkim might hog the headlines, but from Yorkshire to Macedonia, Vancouver to Antarctica, there's a globe-spanning range of recommendations.

Picking the best in travel each year is a delicious and agonising process, with a

JONATHAN GRIFFITH / AURORA PHOTOS · CORBIS ©

shortlist made of suggestions from our authors, staff and community and voted on by a panel of travel-hardened hacks including Lonely Planet co-founder Tony Wheeler. For most places we've chosen there's a strong reason to go this year, be it a sporting event or a revitalised infrastructure, while there are a few we couldn't resist including because they just have that aura of 'right now' about them.

In addition to the top 30 places to visit this year, we've also included a selection of travel lists which should give you a few fresh ideas, whether you're looking to mark an unusual anniversary, discover the world according to the Beatles or Shakespeare, try out the trendiest boot camps, or pinch the pennies with our eagerly anticipated best-value destinations.

If you agree with us, the question is where to go first. If not, feel free to tell us where we've led you astray. Either way, a fabulous year on the road awaits.

Tom Hall, Lonely Planet Travel Editor

LONELY PLANET'S

TOP 10

COUNTRIES

> 'Brazil's diversity will leave you slack-jawed every time you tear yourself away from the beach or jungle'

NORTH AMERICA

EUROPE

ASIA

AFRICA

SOUTH AMERICA ○ **BRAZIL**

AUSTRALIA

ANTARCTICA

#1

BRAZIL

ADVENTURE EVENTS FOOD

by Kevin Raub

- ✪ **POPULATION** 201 million
- ✪ **FOREIGN VISITORS PER YEAR** 5.7 million (2012)
- ✪ **CAPITAL** Brasília
- ✪ **LANGUAGE** Portuguese
- ✪ **MAJOR INDUSTRIES** Agriculture, mining, manufacturing
- ✪ **UNIT OF CURRENCY** Real (R$)
- ✪ **COST INDEX** Espresso R$3-5 (US$1.50-2.50), *caipirinha* on the beach R$10 (US$5), Série A football match R$40-130 (US$20-65)

WHY GO IN 2014?
ALL EYES ON THE PITCH

As if endless strands of sun-toasted coast, mountains splashed with Crayola-green rainforest and significant populations of some the planet's most beautiful colonial villages and wildlife didn't already add up to an unfair share of heaven, Brazil goes and snags two of the most coveted sporting events in the world, beginning with the 2014 FIFA World Cup and followed two years later by the 2016 Summer Olympics. Tack on a recession-dodging economy, and boom! Brazil is the belle of the ball.

Of course, hosting two of the world's most high-profile events means Brazil's infrastructure and security have come under scrutiny, and – despite some occasional lapses – both are on track to ensure a smooth ride to visitors in 2014. Rio de Janeiro has made huge strides in crime crackdown and now offers a palpable sense of security along world-famous sands such as Copacabana, Ipanema and Leblon; other FIFA World Cup host cities such as São Paulo, Belo Horizonte, Recife and Manaus are following suit.

While the focal point of these events will be Rio – where idyllic golden beaches, iconic postcard-perfect mountains and one of the sexiest populations on the planet create an intoxicating tropical cocktail that leaves visitors punch-drunk on paradise – Brazil, despite the stereotypes, is much more than beaches and bikinis.

After joining the *caipirinha*-fuelled caravans in FIFA World Cup host cities, an

IT'S ALL GLITTER AND FEATHERS FOR THE CARNAVAL PARADE IN RIO DE JANEIRO'S SAMBADROME

escape will be in order. Be it trekking across towering windswept dunes peppered with cerulean lagoons in Lençóis Maranhenses, exploring gilded colonial churches in frozen-in-time cities such as Ouro Preto or swimming in aquarium-like rivers near Bonito, Brazil's diversity will leave you slack-jawed every time you tear yourself away from the beach or jungle.

LIFE-CHANGING EXPERIENCES

Brazil's list of dream destinations is long. Rio's urban setting is the southern hemisphere's most stunning, while a visit to the iconic Iguaçu Falls – where 275 waterfalls crash across the border with Argentina – is simply unforgettable. And then there's the enigmatic Amazon and wildlife-rich Pantanal, two of the most biodiverse regions on earth.

RECENT FAD

The country's gastronomic capital, São Paulo, has embraced gourmet street-food fairs. Events such as O Mercado (monthly in Vila Mariana) and Feirinha Gastronômica (weekly in Vila Madalena) feature booth after booth of local chefs whipping up delicious culinary offerings to salivating *paulistanos*. And the food-truck craze is on its way to Brazil – just as soon as most cities can work out hygiene legislation.

HOT TOPIC OF THE DAY

Redemption. To say that the pressure on O Seleção, as Brazil's national football team is known locally, has been ratcheted up to stratospheric levels would be the understatement of the decade. In 1950, the last time Brazil hosted the FIFA World Cup, it bowed out in the final to Uruguay at Rio's newly built Maracanã stadium in heartbreaking fashion – something no Brazilian has forgotten to this day.

REGIONAL FLAVOURS

No South American country can match the diversity and cultural pedigree of Brazil's local grub. In the north, indigenous Amazonian ingredients such as *tucupi* and *jambu* shape local dishes of duck and river fish. African roots fuel the cuisine of the northeast, where *vatapá* (a paste of shrimp, coconut milk and peanuts) stuffed inside *acarajé* (fried fritters made from black-eyed peas) makes for Bahia's ultimate cross-continental snack. Brazil's two most famous dishes, *moqueca* (spicy seafood stew) and *feijoada* (bean stew with pork or beef), are also steeped in African influences. In São Paulo, Japanese, Italian, Syrian and Lebanese immigrants have introduced delectable ethnic cuisine. And in the south, cowboy culture – and beef – rules.

✺ Festivals & Events

✪ Some six million revellers converge amid sun, sand and samba during Rio de Janeiro's annual Carnaval celebrations from 28 February to 4 March.

✪ From 12 June to 13 July, the world's biggest football party comes to Brazil. The 2014 FIFA World Cup kicks off in São Paulo and ends in Rio de Janeiro a month later, hitting 10 additional cities in between.

'It's a chance to take life on and follow in the path of other intrepid explorers'

○ ANTARCTICA

ANTARCTICA

 | |

ACTIVITIES   ADVENTURE   OFF-ROAD

by Alexis Averbuck

- **✪ FOREIGN VISITORS PER YEAR** Tourists 26,509, staff 2468, ship crew 14,652; summer scientists and logistics support 4500
- **✪ CAPITAL** None
- **✪ LANGUAGES** Many
- **✪ MAJOR INDUSTRIES** Science and tourism; in the Southern Ocean, fishing
- **✪ UNIT OF CURRENCY** Shipboard currency, usually US dollars, Euros or British pounds; bases use national currency or US dollars
- **✪ COST INDEX** Ten-day voyage from US$5000, 20-day voyage from US$12,750; flight to the South Pole US$45,000; guided climb of Mt Vinson US$39,900

WHY GO IN 2014? THE ADVENTURE OF A LIFETIME

Tune into your average wildlife television program and you can't fail to be dazzled by Antarctica's majestic icebergs, calving glaciers and unexplored mountain ranges. Or you'll watch its native penguin species frolic while avoiding fierce leopard seals and roaming pods of killer whales, as millions of seabirds spiral over the wild Southern Ocean. It's inspiring stuff.

Visiting this pristine continent (which doesn't have an indigenous population and is not actually a country) in 2014 is a chance to take life on and follow in the path of other intrepid explorers – but with cushier amenities. Reaching the ends of the earth has never been easier but it's not a trip for the weak of heart or stomach: the Drake Passage is a notorious churner.

Two years after the centenary of Scott's and Amundsen's historic trips to the Pole and the BBC's television series, *Frozen Planet*, this year marks the centenary of the start of Ernest Shackleton's infamous attempted Antarctic crossing. During this epic journey Shackleton's ship, *Endurance*, became ice-locked, setting off a hair-raising series of events. A century later and the cruise ships that depart Tierra del Fuego for the continent must adhere to strict safety guidelines and all visitors must follow a code of conduct designed to protect the wildlife.

Clearly, there's no eco-friendly way to visit this fragile environment. There's plenty you can read about the effects of climate change on the world's southernmost land. But there's also an argument for experiencing Antarctica directly because being there brings home to you the significance of this remarkable place.

EMPEROR PENGUINS AT SNOW HILL ISLAND, ANTARCTIC PENINSULA

LIFE-CHANGING EXPERIENCES

Antarctica and its surrounding islands offer the wildest, most remote spots on earth. Immerse yourself in the isolation, the vast expanses of ice and ocean, and the sheer majesty of being a dot in a powerful landscape. Spot minke whales breaching by your ship, spy on Adélie penguins breeding in massive rookeries, and listen for glaciers shearing into the sea. Go exploring from the 'Banana Belt' (the warmer Antarctic Peninsula) to its furthest, coldest reaches, high on the Polar Plateau. Investigate historic huts in the Ross Sea area, and visit active bases on the Peninsula doing cutting-edge scientific research. Don't neglect the islands: on South Georgia Island elephant seals defend their terrain, and Grytviken is tops for whaling history. Visit volcanic Deception Island in the South Shetlands for the chance to bathe in thermal waters. Or get wild: some expeditions provide kayaks, guided hikes, or trips to the interior, even the Holy Grail: the South Pole.

RECENT FAD

The Antarctic explorers' centenaries have brought an upsurge in private expeditions. The deep-pocketed or the well-connected, from Al Gore and Sir Richard Branson to Sir Ranulph Fiennes, have visited the world's wildest continent, raising awareness about climate change, raising cash for charity, or turning back, frostbitten.

WHAT'S HOT...

Responsible travel, BBC's *Frozen Planet*, retracing explorers' routes

...WHAT'S NOT

Crowding penguins for a photo op, rising sea levels worldwide

HOT TOPIC OF THE DAY

Science. Antarctica's cold, undisturbed atmosphere provides an excellent environment for studying the universe, and some of the world's most high-tech work is in the offing here. Snazzy telescopes watch the stars, while IceCube, a 1-sq-km buried array of sensors beneath the Pole, detects neutrinos travelling through the ice. Interdisciplinary projects study everything from the melting ice and climate change (using ice cores) to the creatures in the coldest parts of the ocean. Recently, scientists have begun exploring subglacial lakes such as Lake Vostok, cut off from the atmosphere for 20 million years, and they are remote-mapping the Gamburtsev Mountains – a range the size of the Alps, buried beneath the ice.

MOST BIZARRE SIGHTS

Atmospheric phenomena: aurora australis, nacreous clouds, Fata Morgana and sun dogs.

⊛ SCOTLAND

NORTH AMERICA

EUROPE

ASIA

AFRICA

AMERICA

AUSTRALIA

'Fall in love with the landscape that inspired poet Robert Burns'

ANTARCTICA

SCOTLAND

ACTIVITIES   EVENTS   CULTURE

by Dan Savery Raz

⊛ **POPULATION** 5.3 million

⊛ **FOREIGN VISITORS PER YEAR** 2.35 million

⊛ **CAPITAL** Edinburgh

⊛ **LANGUAGES** English, Scots (Lallans), Scottish Gaelic

⊛ **MAJOR INDUSTRIES** Energy, finance, tourism

⊛ **UNIT OF CURRENCY** British pound (£)

⊛ **COST INDEX** Double room in B&B £60 (US$90), haggis with neeps and tatties £11 (US$16), glass of malt whisky £3.50 (US$5.30), entry to Edinburgh Castle £16 (US$24)

WHY GO IN 2014?
IT'S AN EVENTFUL YEAR

Glasgow hosts the XX Commonwealth Games in the summer of 2014. This major sporting event brings thousands of people from the 71 nations of the former British Empire to Scotland. To coincide with the Games, Glasgow has had a multimillion-pound facelift. The city has never looked so good, with new sports venues such as the Sir Chris Hoy Velodrome, improved transport links and a regeneration of Glasgow Harbour, home to the ultramodern Riverside Museum.

It is also the Year of Homecoming, a government initiative to welcome the Scottish diaspora back to the mother country by celebrating Scotland's heritage, food and drink. The phrase 'there's something for everyone' applies: Europe's biggest brass band festival blasts Perthshire and there will be an orienteering contest around Scottish castles. Local food and drink is showcased at the Spirit of Speyside Whisky Festival in May.

Despite all this, politics will take centre stage: to be or not to be independent, that is the question. This year, three centuries after the Act of Union which created the UK, the Scots finally decide. The referendum on independence is set for 18 September, and politicians will be battling to win Scottish hearts in the build-up to the big vote.

And then there are the Highland Games, the Ryder Cup at Gleneagles and Edinburgh's Festival. Hold onto your hats, Scotland…

A RED DEER STAG ROAMS GLEN GARRY BEFORE SGURR MOR IN SCOTLAND'S HIGHLANDS

LIFE-CHANGING EXPERIENCES

Ascend Arthur's Seat, an outstanding grassy peak in Holyrood Park, for panoramic views of Castle Rock looming over Edinburgh – the most gothic city outside Transylvania. Stop for a wee whisky and some fine dining at the Witchery on the Royal Mile before delving into the city's dungeons. Then take the high road to Loch Lomond, Loch Ness and Cairngorms National Park and fall in love with the landscape that inspired poet Robert Burns.

RECENT FAD

Wind farms. Scotland's fastest-growing renewable energy is wind power. By 2020 Scotland aims to generate all of its electricity from renewables, and huge wind farms can be found in Whitelee, Forth and South Ayrshire, with more planned offshore. But not everyone loves these turbines. Donald Trump opposed an offshore wind farm in Aberdeen claiming it would spoil the sea views for golfers at his resort. But he couldn't stop the winds of change.

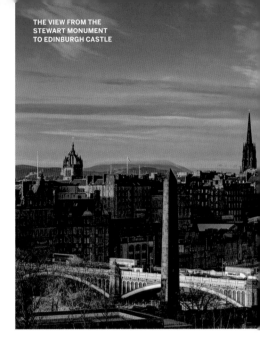

HOT TOPIC OF THE DAY

'Should Scotland be an independent country?' This question, which will be put to Scots in the autumn, has divided opinion. Scotland has had its own parliament since

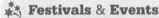

✦ Festivals & Events

✪ Musicians from all over the world jam and jig into the wee hours at Celtic Connections, Glasgow's annual folk, roots and world-music festival held in January and February.

✪ Knights in shining armour are brought to life in a hi-tech, 3D battle at the site of the Battle of Bannockburn, south of Stirling Castle, on 28 and 30 June 2014. The event marks the 700th anniversary of Robert the Bruce's defeat of the English.

✪ The hunt for gold and glory comes to Glasgow (23 July to 3 August) for the XX Commonwealth Games.

✪ The good, the bad and the underworld of music, comedy and theatre invade the capital throughout August for the annual Edinburgh International Festival and its rowdy Fringe.

it devolved in 1999. Alex Salmond, First Minister and leader of the SNP (Scottish National Party), has turned himself into a modern-day William Wallace by calling for independence and whipping up nationalist pride. Yet opposition leaders say Scotland is 'on pause', and Prime Minister David Cameron argues that its military, finance and trade are stronger within the UK.

RANDOM FACTS

✪ The real King Macbeth (whom Shakespeare called the 'Thane of Glamis') did not actually reside at Glamis Castle in Angus, although this is part of the new Macbeth Trail.

✪ Glen Coe, a spectacular Highland valley, is a film star itself, providing backdrops for *Monty Python and the Holy Grail*, *Braveheart* and the third Harry Potter film.

✪ At 1344m above sea level, Ben Nevis (possible translations of the Gaelic include 'venomous', 'dreadful', 'cloudy' or 'heavenly' mountain – take your pick) is the highest point in the British Isles and is a 400-million-year-old, highly eroded, collapsed volcano.

✪ The original kilt was a full-length woven garment that dates back to the 16th century. Supposedly, it was an Englishman who invented the skirt-like 'walking kilt'.

✪ Scottish whisky can be made from malted barley or malted barley with other grains added. The highest form of whisky is a malt whisky from a single distillery; some single malts can be aged 30 years or more. Find out more on the Speyside Malt Whisky Trail and pause at a distillery for a taste.

SWEDEN

NORTH AMERICA · EUROPE · ASIA · AFRICA · SOUTH · RALIA · ANTARCTICA

'The capital has long been a stylish, top-notch destination for serious gourmands and boldly experimental chefs'

#4

SWEDEN

ACTIVITIES CULTURE FOOD

by Becky Ohlsen

- ✪ **POPULATION** 9.6 million
- ✪ **FOREIGN VISITORS PER YEAR** Five million
- ✪ **CAPITAL** Stockholm
- ✪ **LANGUAGES** Swedish; minority languages (Finnish, Meänkieli, Romani Chib, Sámi, Yiddish)
- ✪ **MAJOR INDUSTRIES** Service industry, foreign exports (iron ore, timber, hydropower)
- ✪ **UNIT OF CURRENCY** Krona (Skr)
- ✪ **COST INDEX** Cup of coffee Skr35 (US$5.36), toast Skagen at a Stockholm restaurant Skr155 (US$23.76), hotel double per night Skr1200 (US$183.94), souvenir Dalahäst (wooden horse) from Skr89 (US$13.65)

WHY GO IN 2014? FOOD, CULTURE AND SCARY STORIES

Thanks to the late Swedish author Stieg Larsson's massively popular Millennium trilogy (first the novels, then the film adaptations), as well as equally dark works such as John Ajvide Lindqvist's acclaimed child-vampire romance *Let the Right One In* (also with a film version), we no longer have to explain quite so much about Sweden. These days most people have a sense of what it's like, even in the far north – cold, beautiful and a bit scary. Sweden, in short, is emerging with a new pop-culture persona that has nothing to do with ABBA, meatballs or the Muppets chef.

Perhaps not coincidentally, northern Sweden's largest city, Umeå, is the European Capital of Culture for 2014. If you needed a reason to venture beyond Stockholm and Göteborg, this is a good one.

Then there's the food. The capital has long been a stylish, top-notch destination for serious gourmands and boldly experimental chefs (Stockholm has eight Michelin-starred restaurants), but lately the reputation and influence of Swedish cooking have spread beyond the country's borders. Chef Marcus Samuelsson, who studied in Göteborg and brought his West Coast cooking background to Aquavit in New York, is a well-known example; others include Brooklyn's Aska and,

SWEDEN'S NEW BREED OF CHEFS COOK WITH LOCAL, SEASONAL AND FORAGED INGREDIENTS

at the opposite end of the spectrum, IKEA. Likewise, Swedish groceries (think lingonberry jam, Kalles Kaviar, crispbread, herring, Västerbotten cheese) are showing up more frequently on supermarket shelves abroad. Considering that Swedish cuisine is so strongly tied to locally sourced ingredients (be it seafood, game, berries, herbs or regional cheeses), it makes perfect sense to go to the source of all this fine food.

For Swedes, though, the defining event for 2014 is the September elections. Sweden's political culture is very open and demonstrative; expect to see frequent protests and speeches in public squares, especially on issues such as racism, immigration and economic conditions.

LIFE-CHANGING EXPERIENCES

It's a bit of a trek to reach the Arctic Circle, but it's worth the effort. Lappland, Sweden's northernmost province, is part of the traditional home of the Sámi people. Its vast landscapes are magnificent, winter or summer, but one of the best ways to see them is by dog sled. Outfitters based in Kiruna or Umeå can set you up with a team of huskies, a guide and all the equipment you'll need for an exhilarating journey through the wintry flatlands. If you time it right (try for April), you might be lucky enough to spend the days mushing sled dogs and the nights admiring the northern lights. Lappland also offers the chance to try Sámi cuisine, which is based on reindeer meat (cured, roasted, dried, smoked or as sausage) and native berries.

HOT TOPICS OF THE DAY

The final composition of Sweden's ice hockey team for the 2014 Winter Olympic Games in Russia; the hockey-obsessed Swedes are solid gold medal prospects.

RANDOM FACTS

☻ Sweden is 53% forest.
☻ The average number of people per square kilometre is 23.
☻ All Swedish employers are required to provide free massages for employees.

✯✯ Festivals & Events

☻ Immerse yourself in traditional Sámi culture during Ubmejen Biejvieh (Sámi Week), held from 1 to 9 March. There will be music, handicrafts, lectures, performances, food and drink and outdoor activities at Västerbottens Museum and around Umeå.

☻ In May, some of Europe's premier chefs compete in the annual Bocuse d'Or Europe, the European Cuisine Contest. It's held this year in Stockholm as part of GastroNord, northern Europe's biggest hotel and restaurant trade show.

☻ Midsummer's Eve and Midsummer's Day are Sweden's main summer holidays, with lots of eating, drinking, singing and dancing around maypoles; this year they're on 20 and 21 June.

☻ A one-stop shop for music fans, the annual Way Out West festival rocks Göteborg from 14 to 16 August 2014.

'This slip of a country has so far escaped the safari-suited "bush and beach" crowd'

NORTH AMERICA

EUROPE

ASIA

AFRICA

SOUTH AMERICA

✪ **MALAWI**

AUSTRALIA

ANTARCTICA

#5

MALAWI

ACTIVITIES ADVENTURE OFF-ROAD

by Nana Luckham

- ✪ **POPULATION** 15.4 million
- ✪ **FOREIGN VISITORS PER YEAR** 750,000
- ✪ **CAPITAL** Lilongwe
- ✪ **LANGUAGES** Chichewa, English
- ✪ **MAJOR INDUSTRIES** Tobacco, sugar, tea
- ✪ **UNIT OF CURRENCY** Malawian kwacha (MK)
- ✪ **COST INDEX** Bottle of Kuche Kuche beer MK250 (US$0.75), tent site at Majete Community Campsite/cabin at Mkulumadzi Camp MK3250 (US$10)/MK120,000 (US$370) in Majete Wildlife Reserve, PADI Open Water Diver course at Lake Malawi MK127,000 (US$390)

WHY GO IN 2014? THE BIG FIVE & BEACH LIFE WITHOUT THE CROWDS

Picture this: mere hours after touching down in Malawi's second-largest city, Blantyre, you check into superluxe digs (or pitch your tent) at the Majete Wildlife Reserve, which only 10 years ago lay decimated by poaching, but last year gained Big Five status thanks to a wildlife relocation project. You get up close to the aforementioned elephant, rhino, lion, leopard and buffalo without the pesky 4WD scrum so common in Africa's best-known parks.

Then perhaps it's off to Lake Malawi for a spot of high-visibility snorkelling through fluttering clouds of multicoloured fish – think Maldives without the threat of sharks or all-inclusive buffets. Or head for

Mt Mulanje (currently under consideration by Unesco for a World Heritage Site designation) for a hike over hazy peaks in an otherworldly moonscape. And there's always the Viphya Plateau, a haunting wilderness of grasslands and whaleback hills that feels downright prehistoric.

Best get in there quick. Once the preserve of backpackers and gap-year volunteers, this slip of a country has so far escaped the safari-suited 'bush and beach' crowd that flocks to Kenya, Tanzania and Zambia. But international media attention has been rolling in of late, spurred on by the country's revitalised parks and reserves, the beauty and diversity of the lake and the ever-increasing range of lodgings aimed at wallets both big and small.

WILDLIFE-WATCHING WITHOUT THE CROWDS IS A DRAWCARD IN MALAWI

LIFE-CHANGING EXPERIENCES

☼ Travelling down Lake Malawi on the creaking *Ilala* ferry, sleeping in a cosy cabin or out on deck and stopping at fishing villages and islands along the way.

☼ Following in the footsteps of Malawi's early missionaries and hiking to Livingstonia in the north – the Rift Valley unfurls endlessly below you at this beautifully preserved colonial hilltop town.

☼ Gliding scarily close to hippos and crocodiles by boat on the Shire River in Liwonde National Park.

HOT TOPIC OF THE DAY

Joyce Banda, who became the second female leader in Africa in 2012, has made headlines for her fierce defence of women's rights, her devaluation of the national currency and her pledge to overturn the country's ban on homosexuality. A much-publicised email lambasting pop queen Madonna (who has adopted two children from Malawi) for her starry behaviour, her bullying of Malawian officials and her failure to perform 'decent music' turned out to have been written by Banda's press officer.

RANDOM FACTS

☼ In the 1800s the lakeside town of Nkhotakota was home to a huge slave market from which thousands were shipped annually across the lake to Tanzania.

☼ Lake Malawi is home to more than 600 species of fish – more than any other inland body of water in the world.

☼ There are nine national parks and reserves in Malawi, all small by African

standards – the largest, Nyika National Park, is 3000 sq km and home to antelope and lots of leopards.

☼ On sleepy Likoma Island sits a massive Anglican cathedral said to be the same size as England's Winchester Cathedral.

☼ Malawi's longest-ruling leader was the authoritarian Hastings Kamuzu Banda, who presided over Malawi and its predecessor state, Nyasaland, from 1963 to 1994.

☼ The staple food of Malawi is *nsima*, a thick starchy porridge made from corn, cassava or other starch flour.

☼ Malawi is one of the poorest countries in the world – more than 70% of the population lives on less than US$1 a day.

MOST BIZARRE SIGHT

It's a crisp spring morning and you're in the mist-soaked Scottish Highlands, skipping past glistening lakes and carpets of wildflowers. Oh wait! There's a zebra. And is that a leopard lurking in the trees? Turns out you're in Malawi's Nyika National Park – a 3200-sq-km wilderness area that's part Scotland, part Yorkshire moors, but with more exotic wildlife thrown in.

> 'Mexico's image is on the cusp of change –
> it's time to dust off your Mexican dream
> again and enjoy it to the max'

MEXICO

#6

MEXICO

ACTIVITIES CULTURE FOOD

by John Noble

- **POPULATION** 116 million
- **FOREIGN VISITORS PER YEAR** 23 million
- **CAPITAL** Mexico City
- **LANGUAGES** Spanish, about 70 indigenous languages
- **MAJOR INDUSTRY** Food and drinks
- **UNIT OF CURRENCY** Peso (M$)
- **COST INDEX** Midrange double room M$500-1200 (US$41-99), small-car rental per day M$500-600 (US$41-49), taco M$10-25 (US$0.80-2), Pacific coast whale-watching M$400-500 (US$33-41)

WHY GO IN 2014? THE SLEEPING GIANT IS WAKING

Sunbaking on a Caribbean beach after partying all night in Cancún; shopping for brightly coloured handicrafts or gorging on seven types of *mole* (chilli sauce) in Oaxaca; stepping back in time at a Mayan temple – it's easy to feel optimistic when you're kicking back in Mexico. And it's not just the holidaymakers who are feeling that way. All of a sudden, there's a new air of positivity in and around Mexico.

If there was a single turning point, it was the arrival of a new president, Enrique Peña Nieto, in December 2012. Peña Nieto, of the once deeply discredited PRI (Institutional Revolutionary Party), was far from every Mexican's choice for president. But most people welcomed his pragmatic approach, and early actions to improve education standards and increase competition suggested that Peña Nieto might deliver on his promises of change. The economy has been growing even faster than Brazil's, and there are even indications that drug-trade-related crime – concentrated in specific areas, with no impact on the vast majority of visitors – is on the way down. Many Mexicans are happier about living in Mexico now than most can ever remember: the flow of emigrants to the USA may soon be exceeded by those returning home.

But Mexico's road back began before Peña Nieto took office. The economy had already started rebounding in 2010 and of course Mexico's myriad attractions never

THE MUSEO DE ARTE MODERNO IN CHAPULTEPEC PARK, MEXICO CITY, INCLUDES WORKS BY FRIDA KAHLO AND DIEGO RIVERA

went away. Exciting developments on the travel scene have continued, from major new Maya museums in Cancún and Mérida to the installation of Latin America's longest ziplines on the rim of the awe-inspiring Copper Canyon. Hip boutique hotels are being established in beautiful colonial buildings and there's a blossoming contemporary art scene in Mexico City.

Now Mexico's image is on the cusp of change – it's time to dust off your Mexican dream again and enjoy it to the max before those prices go back up and the crowds really start rolling in.

LIFE-CHANGING EXPERIENCES

You can bliss out in a hammock with a bottle of Bohemia beer and the Pacific Ocean breaking metres away – or climb out of your hammock to surf the legendary Mexican Pipeline at Puerto Escondido and dive the stunning coral reefs of the Caribbean coast. Venture inland to climb the Maya temples of Palenque with howler monkeys roaring in the jungle. Relive Frida Kahlo's anguished existence among her art in her Mexico City

home. And discover that Mexican food is not just chili con carne and burritos, but has as many varieties as there are Mexican cooks, from tacos filled with the northwest's delicious *carne asada* (marinated grilled beef) to Oaxaca's *mole* sauces subtly flavoured with seasonal herbs and spices.

WHAT'S HOT...

Urban cycling, slowly sipping quality tequila or mezcal

...WHAT'S NOT

Gas-guzzling automobiles, chucking back endless shots of industrial-quality liquor

RANDOM FACTS

✪ Cholula's Tepanapa Pyramid is the world's second-biggest pyramid (after Egypt's Pyramid of Cheops), but it looks like a hill with a church on top.

✪ Mexican Carlos Slim Helú is the world's richest man. *Forbes* estimated the net worth of Slim and his family in 2013 at US$73 billion.

✪ El Tri (short for El Tricolor) is the common name for the Mexican flag, the national soccer team, and a veteran 1968 rock band.

✦ Festivals & Events

✪ The 2014 Carnaval happens during the week leading up to 5 March. It's wildest in Veracruz and Mazatlán, with flamboyant, noisy parades and masses of music, drink, dancing, fireworks and fun.

✪ The beautiful colonial city of Oaxaca will be thronged for its fantastically colourful feast of regional dance, the Guelaguetza, on 21 and 28 July.

✪ Cemeteries come alive for the happy-sad remembrance of departed loved ones that is Día de Muertos (Day of the Dead; 2 November). Families decorate graves and commune with their dead, some holding all-night vigils. It's most atmospheric in and around the colonial towns of Pátzcuaro and Oaxaca.

'With such a dreamlike setting, this magical archipelago is a great spot to decompress with a loved one'

○ SEYCHELLES

#7

SEYCHELLES

ACTIVITIES

VALUE

CULTURE

by Jean-Bernard Carillet

- ○ **POPULATION** 90,000
- ○ **FOREIGN VISITORS PER YEAR** 195,000
- ○ **CAPITAL** Victoria
- ○ **LANGUAGES** Creole, English, French
- ○ **MAJOR INDUSTRIES** Tourism, fishing, financial services
- ○ **UNIT OF CURRENCY** Seychelles rupee (Rs)
- ○ **COST INDEX** Ice-cold Seybrew beer Rs 30 (US$2.60), double in a self-catering apartment Rs 1500 (US$130), single dive Rs 650 (US$56), catch-of-the-day fish Rs 160 (US$14)

WHY GO IN 2014?
PARADISE WITHIN REACH

These 115 divine islands strewn across the peacock-blue Indian Ocean have all the key ingredients for a once-in-a-lifetime holiday, but their reputation as a millionaire's playground may have kept you away. Good news: this paradise has never been so easily accessible. On top of exclusive island hideaways and elegant ecovillas synonymous with barefoot luxury, you can benefit from the wallet-friendlier B&Bs, picturesque Creole guesthouses and self-catering apartments that have sprung up over the past decade. Although the Seychelles remains a chic destination, local tourist authorities are now promoting these economy options. And if expensive air tickets deterred you from visiting, rejoice! The situation has dramatically changed over the past few years due to increased competition. Most airlines based in the Gulf, including Emirates, Qatar Airways and Etihad, have launched frequent, well-priced services to the Seychelles from their respective hubs, offering excellent connections with major capitals worldwide. Your dollars or euros have never gone so much further – now is the time to delve in.

What to expect? Believe the hype: the Seychelles has some of the most alluring beaches in the southern hemisphere. Many think the eye-catching brochure images of turquoise seas and shimmering white sands are digitally enhanced but, once there, they realise the pictures barely do

PALM TREES RING A
SECLUDED BEACH HAVEN
ON PRASLIN ISLAND

✦✦ Festivals & Events

☀ International Carnival of Victoria is held from 25 to 27 April on Mahé. You'll find extravagant parades, parties, concerts, street performances and fireworks. It's a recent festival (since 2011), so you can expect lots of commitment from the population and fresh vibes.

☀ October is the time of the colourful and vibrant Festival Kreol, the Seychelles' premier festival, held every year during the last week of the month. A celebration of Creole heritage, it's an explosion of local cuisine, theatre, art, music, street processions and dance.

☀ Calling all divers and photographers! Subios Underwater Festival is a three-day-long underwater film and image festival held in the last week of November on Mahé. Now's your chance to see that whale shark with its mouth wide open!

them justice. With such a dreamlike setting, this magical archipelago is, unsurprisingly, a great spot to decompress with a loved one. But there's much more to do than simply sipping cocktails on the beach. Hiking, diving, snorkelling, boat tours and other adventure options are all readily available, with the added appeal of grandiose scenery. Wildlife lovers will get a buzz too – the Seychelles is not dubbed 'The Galápagos of the Indian Ocean' for nothing. Scratch the neck of a giant tortoise, swim alongside a photogenic whale shark or observe tens of thousands of nesting sooty terns. The best part is, you don't need a telelens to capture such scenes.

LIFE-CHANGING EXPERIENCE

There's no shortage of photogenic beaches in the Seychelles, but Anse Source d'Argent, on the island of La Digue, is an all-time favourite. This is the tropical paradise you've always dreamt about: a dazzling white powdery sand beach framed by naturally sculpted granite boulders and lapped by topaz waters. Another staggeringly sexy beach is Anse Lazio, on Praslin. The long, broad, pale-sand beach has lapis-lazuli waters on one side and a thick fringe of palm trees on the other, with a series of glacis rocks at each end.

RANDOM FACTS

☀ Aldabra Atoll, the world's largest raised coral atoll and a Unesco World Heritage Site and nature reserve, is home to about 150,000 giant tortoises.
☀ On Frégate Island, the giant tenebrionid beetle is a 4cm-long insect that's apparently found nowhere else on earth.
☀ Fruit bat is considered a delicacy in the Seychelles and is served in selected restaurants.

MOST BIZARRE SIGHT

This must be the sexiest fruit on earth, and it could be mistaken for some kind of erotic gadgetry in a sex shop. The *coco fesse* (the fruit of the coco de mer palm) looks like, ahem, a pair of buttocks. Praslin's World Heritage–listed Vallée de Mai is one of only two places in the world where you can see the rare coco de mer palms growing in their natural state.

● **BELGIUM**
EUROPE

NORTH
AMERICA

ASIA

AFRICA

'Belgo-newbies will find medieval towns where culture and gastronomy meet'

AUSTRALIA

ANTARCTICA

#8

BELGIUM

EVENTS   CULTURE   FOOD

by Oliver Bennett

● **POPULATION** 11 million

● **FOREIGN VISITORS PER YEAR** 7.5 million (2011)

● **CAPITAL** Brussels

● **LANGUAGES** Dutch (Flemish), French, German

● **MAJOR INDUSTRIES** Wide-ranging, from pharmaceuticals to financial services

● **UNIT OF CURRENCY** Euro (€)

● **COST INDEX** Cup of coffee €2 (US$2.70), a beer €2-4.50 (US$2.70-6), midrange hotel double or B&B per night €60-140 (US$80-190), short taxi ride €5 (US$6.50), 500g box of top-end pralines from Mary in Brussels €34 (US$45)

WHY GO IN 2014?
FOR HIGH EMOTIONS
IN THE LOW COUNTRY

Belgium has picturesque cities – Bruges, Antwerp, Ghent – and in Brussels a walkable capital with great museums. The food and drink is a gustatory blast (think the world's best beer, chocolate and chips), the countryside flat and placid, the seaside surprisingly chic, while cultural treasures range from medieval masters to Tintin. Yet the words 'Belgium' and 'holiday' don't usually mix. From 2014, a huge influx of visitors is expected due to the 100th anniversary of the outbreak of WWI – a festival of remembrance lasting until 2018 – which may change preconceptions.

Belgo-newbies will find medieval towns where culture and gastronomy meet, with Gothic buildings, paintings by Breugel, Van Eyck and Magritte, canals and cool shops. And they'll discover mellow meadows, where cows moo beside monuments, and battlefields and cemeteries that testify to the horrors of a war now shifting from living memory. In the northwest of Flanders, the country's northern region, fields became battlegrounds, villages were destroyed, millions were killed or went missing. Perhaps this four-year commemoration will break WWI's baleful spell forever.

LIFE-CHANGING
EXPERIENCES

✪ Handsome and rebuilt, the town of Ypres – 'Wipers' to English-speaking soldiers – is agreeable. But it's also the epicentre of the WWI trauma and home to

CISTERCIAN MONKS MAKE BEER AT THE CHIMAY BREWERY, SCOURMONT ABBEY

the Menin Gate memorial to the missing. By day this monument is part of the main thoroughfare, while every night since 1928 the road has closed at 8pm for a Last Post ceremony, providing a simple, poignant focus for those 'never again' sentiments.

✪ Don't miss the food in Belgium. 'French food in German portions', they say. Fish or chicken *waterzooi* (a soupy stew) is delicious, and in season you'll find *moules-frites* (mussels with chips) everywhere – Belgian chips are double-fried for extra crispness. Also look out for grey shrimps, harvested in coastal Koksijde. Belgium has more Michelin-starred restaurants per capita than France, and more than 400 kinds of beer including the superb if ultra-rare Westvleteren 12, voted the world's best beer by RateBeer three times since 2005.

WHAT'S HOT...
Beer made by Trappist monks, late-night cones of *frites* and mayo, Jacques Brel

---

...WHAT'S NOT
Constant pro- and anti-EU arguments, the Manneken Pis statue in Brussels

---

HOT TOPIC OF THE DAY
Belgium has a monarchy, a football team and borders, but many think of it as two

- Brussels is the capital of the EU and houses the headquarters of NATO.
- The longest tramway line in the world is the Belgian Coast Tram at 68km.
- The saxophone was named after its Belgian inventor, Adolphe Sax.

MOST BIZARRE SIGHT

The country that gave us René Magritte is full of surreal surprises, but the Atomium – a gigantic metallic ball-and-stick lattice built in Brussels for the 1958 World's Fair – takes the waffle. A retro treat.

✦ Festivals & Events

- Over the next four years, many events will revolve around the WWI theme. In Brussels an oratorio for peace premieres in November 2014, with choristers from 35 Belgian choirs and representatives of 35 nations that were involved in the war.

- Antwerp hosts a wide range of commemorative WWI activities based around three themes – historical narrative, avant-garde art and refugees – starting from 3 to 5 October 2014 with a temporary, army-built pontoon across the Scheldt River.

- The Zythos Beer Festival is the largest in Belgium and now takes place near Leuven; the 2014 dates are 22 to 28 April. Expect more than 400 styles of beer and lashings of fun.

- Prefer some music with your beer? The Pukkelpop festival takes place every year in August near Hasselt.

countries. In recent years, differences between Dutch-speaking Flanders in the north and French-speaking Wallonia in the south have become marked. So much so, in fact, that the schism which started in 2007 led to a national deadlock lasting for 541 days – the world-record time for a modern country to go without a government. Just passing through? Be sensitive. Learn a word or two of both Dutch and French.

RANDOM FACTS

- Antwerp is the world's key diamond centre – almost 90% of the globe's raw diamonds pass through.

NORTH
AMERICA

EUROPE
⊙ **MACEDONIA**

ASIA

AFRICA

SOUTH

AUSTRALIA

ANTARCTICA

'Macedonia's mix of history and uncharted outdoors offers a uniquely cultured kind of adrenaline rush'

MACEDONIA

ADVENTURE OFF-ROAD CULTURE

by Chris Deliso

- ⊙ **POPULATION** Two million
- ⊙ **FOREIGN VISITORS PER YEAR** 700,000
- ⊙ **CAPITAL** Skopje
- ⊙ **LANGUAGES** Macedonian; also Albanian, Romani, Serbian and Turkish on local levels
- ⊙ **MAJOR INDUSTRIES** Food processing, textiles, construction
- ⊙ **UNIT OF CURRENCY** Macedonian denar (MKD)
- ⊙ **COST INDEX** Small bottle of local wine 250-400MKD (US$5-8.50), lake/river trout (entrée) 350MKD (US$7.40), barbershop haircut 60-200MKD (US$1.30-4.25), transport and guide for deep powder skiing at 2500m per day for 10 people 12,000MKD (US$255)

WHY GO IN 2014?
BACK TO THE FUTURE,
BALKAN-STYLE

The year 2014 marks the completion of the government's love-it-or-hate-it makeover of the capital, Skopje. Adding to the existing mix of eclectic former Yugoslav construction and Ottoman relics, this civic plan includes walking bridges and statues of randy bulls, fierce lions, trendy gals, Byzantine emperors, medieval tsars and – at the very centre of the main square – a massive Alexander the Great on horseback, set atop a splendid, multicoloured fountain where naughty kids take a swipe at soaking their parents.

While urban renewal has hogged all the limelight, the Macedonian capital has at the same time quietly become more visitor-friendly, with an inexpensive new airport–city shuttle (finally!), a bevy of cool new hostels, upscale wine bars and bistros, and one of southeastern Europe's best club scenes. The city's new structures also include a Holocaust Memorial Centre that celebrates the culture of Macedonia's largely vanished Sephardic Jewish community, decimated in WWII.

Beyond work-in-progress Skopje and the more established tourist sites such as Lake Ohrid, Mavrovo ski area and ancient Stobi, new things are happening elsewhere. Quiet Berovo, on the border with Bulgaria, is an up-and-coming contender on the spa-hotel scene. Also in Macedonia's idyllic eastern half, sturdy old Kratovo – with Ottoman-era stone bridges and cobblestone lanes – is revitalising previously derelict Turkish

THE CHURCH OF SVETI
JOVAN AT KANEO ON THE
SHORES OF LAKE OHRID

mansions, attesting the bygone wealth of this old mining town. And in the arid central vineyard region of Tikveš, new quality wineries are catering to thirsty visitors.

LIFE-CHANGING EXPERIENCES

For the adventurous traveller, Macedonia's mix of history and uncharted outdoors offers a uniquely cultured kind of adrenaline rush. Although there's a ski resort with plenty of powder at Popova Šapka in the northwest, off-piste skiing here (at 2500m) is available with a local guide and a day's use of a lumbering snowcat to get to the furthest reaches.

In warmer months, action seekers can try paragliding from Mt Galičica over vast Lake Ohrid in the southwest. Ohrid is a summer hot spot with a sprawling old town with structures ranging from classical amphitheatres and Byzantine churches to traditional wood-beamed mansions overlooking the lake. And if you're up for a 30km swim, try competing in the summer swimming marathon here.

Further east, in the wild Mariovo region, take a 4WD through the borderland near Greece to hunt for hidden French gold or rusty German battle helmets left over from the Great War. Since there's been talk of gentrifying the region's nearly abandoned traditional villages, or even new industrial projects, get there while it's still pristine.

RECENT FAD

Urban renewal. Inspired by Skopje, smaller cities such as Prilep, Bitola and Strumica are smartening up their own public spaces.

WHAT'S HOT...

Shiny shopping malls, metrosexual fitness centres, Turkish soap operas, political activists sparring on social media

...WHAT'S NOT

Driving an old car, excessive smoking, any desire for future EU membership

HOT TOPICS OF THE DAY

Construction and congestion. Greece and Bulgaria have accused Skopje's 2014 construction project of 'stealing' their historic heroes. Macedonians are more concerned about the effect of new apartment blocks and shopping malls on increasing urban pollution, and planned grandiose hotels that might mar the landscape in touristed areas. Plans for underground bypass roadways and a light-rail system might help the battle against Skopje's chronic smog and traffic.

✫ Festivals & Events

✪ The midwinter Vevčani Carnival (13 and 14 January) transforms this sleepy village into a raucous party zone, replete with locally crafted floats, masked locals, traditional music and plenty of homemade food and firewater, served up for free by the hospitable locals.

✪ From mid-July to mid-August, the Ohrid Summer Festival is a mix of theatre, dance, art, literature and music, performed in acoustically ideal venues such as the Classical Amphitheatre and Sveta Sofija Cathedral.

✪ The perennially popular Skopje Jazz Festival is held in October.

'Hoof it over pitcher plants and granite moonscapes for the ultimate Bornean sunrise'

NORTH AMERICA

EUROPE

ASIA

AFRICA

◉ **MALAYSIA**

SOUTH AMERICA

AUSTRALIA

ANTARCTICA

#10

MALAYSIA

ADVENTURE FOOD FAMILY

by Simon Richmond

- ✪ **POPULATION** 28.8 million
- ✪ **FOREIGN VISITORS PER YEAR** 25 million
- ✪ **CAPITAL** Kuala Lumpur
- ✪ **LANGUAGES** Bahasa Malaysia, English
- ✪ **MAJOR INDUSTRIES** Electronics and electronic goods, palm oil
- ✪ **UNIT OF CURRENCY** Malaysian ringgit (RM)
- ✪ **NUMBER OF SULTANS** Nine
- ✪ **COST INDEX** Cup of coffee RM5 (US$1.65), midrange double room RM100 (US$33), short taxi ride RM10 (US$3.30), internet per hour RM3 (US$1), laksa RM5 (US$1.65)

WHY GO IN 2014?
IT'S VISIT MALAYSIA YEAR

The political upheaval of the 2013 general election is over, so now it's back to business for a country intent on defining itself as 'truly Asia'. The government has a target of 28 million visitors for its Visit Malaysia campaign, three million over the current tally.

Among new tourist attractions are the largest bird park in Southeast Asia, in Melaka (with 6000 birds featuring 400 species), and Legoland Malaysia and Hello Kitty Land in Nusajaya, which are packing in both locals and Singaporeans flocking across the causeway.

The new second terminal at Kuala Lumpur International Airport (KLIA2), catering mainly to the booming budget-airline sector, is another major factor in attracting more visitors. Competitive fares offered by Malaysia Airlines, AirAsia, Firefly and new operator Malindo Air make getting around this widely spread-out country a cinch. Further afield, weekly direct links are now scheduled to destinations as diverse as Istanbul and Pyongyang.

Sabah had some bad press in 2013 following an incursion by scores of Filipinos on a coastal village in the southeast corner of the state. However, there's no problem travelling in the rest of this large region of Malaysian Borneo – experience new sustainable-tourism initiatives in off-the-beaten-track Kudat, or the luxury of Gaya Island Resort on Pulau Gaya within the Tunku Abdul Rahman National Park.

The chaotic building site engulfing KL Sentral, the transport hub of the capital Kuala Lumpur, is beginning to resolve

THE GODDESS OF MERCY TEMPLE IS ONE OF THE OLDEST CHINESE TEMPLES IN GEORGE TOWN, PENANG

itself with new residential, office and hotel towers and malls opening for business. The Aloft Hotel and Nu Sentral Mall are up and running, while later in 2014 the luxurious St Regis Hotel is set to throw open its doors.

LIFE-CHANGING EXPERIENCES

✪ Tuck into delicious street food such as *char kway teow* (flat rice noodles), *assam* laksa (rice noodles in fish broth) and curry *mee* (more noodles) in George Town, Penang.

✪ Experience longhouse life and local hospitality in Sarawak's Kelabit Highlands.

✪ Hoof it over pitcher plants and granite moonscapes for the ultimate Bornean sunrise atop Mt Kinabalu.

✪ Get a bird's-eye view of the jungle from the canopy walkway in Taman Negara, Malaysia's premier national park.

✪ Village-hop, dive, snorkel and jungle-trek on Pulau Tioman.

✪ In March or early April, join fast-car lovers at the Sepang International Circuit for the Malaysian Grand Prix, or bird fanciers for the Raptor Watch Festival at Cape Rachado Forest Reserve near Port Dickson on the Straits of Melaka (usually in early March).

✪ Head to Penang in June for the artsy George Town Festival, and hit the island again in late August for streetside Chinese-opera performances, part of the Hungry Ghost Festival.

✪ Parades and general festivities are par for the course during the National Day celebrations on 31 August; grab a ringside seat for the action in Kuala Lumpur's Merdeka Square.

RECENT FAD

Cycle tourism is beginning to take off with guided tours in Sabah, a proposal to build a bike path around the coast of Penang, and a community project to map out cycle routes around Kuala Lumpur.

HOT TOPIC OF THE DAY

Everyone is watching how the new government will shape up. The results of the most closely contested election in Malaysia's history have been denounced by opposition parties, undermining the ruling party's call for national unity and reconciliation.

RANDOM FACTS

✪ Operating on a rotational cycle, each of Malaysia's nine sultans takes a turn as the country's head of state, serving for a five-year term. The current one is the octogenarian Sultan Abdul Halim of Kedah, who first held the position from 1970 to 1975.

✪ Malaysian contemporary art is hot: artists whose work you should look out for include Ivan Lam, Ahmad Zakii Anwar, Jalaini Abu Hassan, Anurendra Jegadeva and Yee I-Lann, who has made a name for herself with digital art.

MOST BIZARRE SIGHT

During the festival of Thaipusam, held in Kuala Lumpur, Ipoh, Penang and Johor Bahru, you can see religious devotees pierce their skin with spikes and hooks, from which they hang milk pots, decorations and pictures of Hindu deities.

FEAST LIKE A LOCAL WITH A TABLE FULL OF STREET FOOD IN PENANG

LONELY PLANET'S

TOP 10

REGIONS

NORTH AMERICA

EUROPE

ASIA
○ **SIKKIM**

AFRICA

SOUTH

ANTARCTICA

'Simply drive along serene backroads, halting at mountain villages where the way of life has changed little over centuries'

#1

SIKKIM, INDIA

ACTIVITIES   ADVENTURE   FOOD

by Anirban Mahapatra

- ○ **POPULATION** 607,700
- ○ **MAIN TOWN** Gangtok
- ○ **LANGUAGES** English, Hindi, Nepali
- ○ **MAJOR INDUSTRIES** Agriculture, tourism
- ○ **UNIT OF CURRENCY** Indian rupee (₹)
- ○ **COST INDEX** Bottle of Dansberg beer ₹70 (US$1.25), plate of pork *momos* ₹55 (US$1), budget hotel room in Gangtok ₹1100 (US$20), all-inclusive daily trek ₹3300 (US$60)

WHY GO IN 2014? GREEN IS THE COLOUR

Picking up national accolades in 2012 for being India's cleanest state with the most innovative tourism project, Sikkim has set new benchmarks for responsible travel in the country. Checkbox sightseeing has rapidly made way for sustainable community-based tourism in less developed areas, while ecofriendly policies have lent new vigour to the virginal Himalayan wilderness that drapes the region's mountains. Clearly, Sikkim is showing the way for what could be the future of India's tourism industry, and the time to experience it is now.

Food-wise, there's news too. Organic farming is the new mantra in Sikkim and is being promoted in a big way. Much of the produce available in local markets is already gunk-free, and the government proposes to convert Sikkim into a fully organic state very soon. For you, this means eating healthy food, and having an awesome holiday between those scrumptious morsels.

And if you're one of those who've long carped about the tiring road journey to Sikkim, wait till you hear this. With a new airport scheduled to open near Gangtok in 2014, you can now shave off several hours of transit time and fly in directly from major Indian metros. If that isn't cool, what is?

LIFE-CHANGING EXPERIENCES

A paradise for adventurers, Sikkim offers a priceless opportunity to hike in the shadow of Mt Khangchendzonga (8586m), the world's third-highest summit, on the fabulous trek to Goecha La. Those seeking more thrills can raft the wild waters of the Teesta River as it rushes down towards the plains. And if cultural variety is what floats your boat, treat yourself to a vista of vivid murals on Sikkim's new and old buildings, explore intriguing Buddhist monasteries stacked with precious relics, or simply drive along serene backroads, halting at nameless villages with a timeless way of life amid this formidable mountainous landscape.

RECENT FAD

Spending the early evening lounging along Mahatma Gandhi (MG) Marg, central Gangtok's picturesque pedestrianised district, is clearly the *número uno* pastime for the town's laid-back yet impeccably modish youth. And you're welcome to join in.

HOT TOPIC OF THE DAY

In 2011, a killer earthquake wreaked havoc in the remote mountains of North Sikkim. Barely a year later, heavy rains and landslides added to the destruction and trauma. Even as you read this, governmental agencies, NGOs and volunteer organisations are working overtime to reinstate normalcy in the region.

RANDOM FACTS

○ Padmasambhava, the legendary Buddhist guru, regarded Sikkim as one of the last utopias on earth.

 Festivals & Events

○ Masked Buddhist deities and infernal demons come to life in full sartorial splendour during vibrant *chaam* dances that take place across Sikkim in the run-up to Losar (Tibetan New Year) in February/March.

○ Around May/June, monastery towns in the state wake up to a flurry of rituals celebrating Buddha's life during the festival of Saga Dawa.

○ Khangchendzonga, located on Sikkim's border with Nepal, is considered the guardian deity of the state. In August every year, the festival of Pang Lhabsol honours the spirit of the mountain with prayers and dances.

○ Sikkim was a monarchy, ruled by a dynasty of kings called chogyals, until its merger with the dominion of India in 1975.
○ The vulnerable and utterly cute red panda is the state animal of Sikkim.

REGIONAL FLAVOURS

In Sikkim, the yummiest of Tibetan staples come alive vis-à-vis a melange of cuisines from the kitchens of various Himalayan tribes. So choose from succulent pork *momos* (dumplings), steaming *thukpa* (Tibetan noodle soup), *sisnoo* (nettle soup), *ningro* (fiddlehead fern), *gundruk ko jhol* (fermented mustard-leaf soup), *churpi* (dried yak cheese) or some heart-warming *tongba* (local millet beer topped with boiling water), and treat your palate to a volley of awesome flavours on your sojourn in the state.

NOVICE BUDDHIST MONKS
ENJOYING A GAME OF
FOOTBALL AT A SIKKIM
MONASTERY

'Carved by giant gorges, dimpled with deep, cool pools, and home to a coastline that could make Australian eastcoasters weep'

❖ THE KIMBERLEY

#2

THE KIMBERLEY, AUSTRALIA

ACTIVITIES | ADVENTURE | OFF-ROAD

by Lorna Parkes

- ❖ **POPULATION** 37,673 (44% Aboriginal)
- ❖ **MAIN TOWNS** Broome (West Kimberley), Kununurra (East Kimberley)
- ❖ **LANGUAGES** English and various indigenous languages
- ❖ **MAJOR INDUSTRIES** Resources, tourism, healthcare, agriculture
- ❖ **UNIT OF CURRENCY** Australian dollar (A$)
- ❖ **COST INDEX** String of top-quality South Sea pearls A$1 million (US$968,710), homestead double room/campsite per person A$170-365/13-21 (US$164-354/ US$12-20), 4WD hire per day from A$120 (US$116), petrol per litre around A$2 (US$1.94), depending on distance from Broome or Kununurra

WHY GO IN 2014? BEAT THE CROWDS & THE RESOURCES JUGGERNAUTS

When 19th-century explorers pitched themselves unwittingly into Australia's interior in the hope of claiming uncharted territory, much of what they saw must have felt like the Kimberley still feels today: eerily expansive, bizarrely empty and undiscovered. It's one of the most sparsely populated regions on the planet and one of the most starkly beautiful, carved by giant gorges, dimpled with deep, cool pools, and home to a coastline that could make Australian eastcoasters weep.

There's more to this outback beauty than just bush camping, billy tea and beer, though. It's also a region where Aboriginal culture rubs shoulders with exotic Asian influences, traditional landowners negotiate with international resources companies, the rich come to spend their millions on world-class pearls, and celebrities fly in for a luxurious sojourn in the vast open spaces.

For travellers, it's always been a difficult nut to crack: croc-infested, almost impossible to travel around without a 4WD, and mostly inaccessible during the wet season (November to March). Travelling here ain't cheap, and independent touring needs

Festivals & Events

✪ Between March and October, Broome holds its own version of a full-moon party during a monthly natural phenomenon called Staircase to the Moon. Market stalls, local entertainers, deck chairs and picnics will throng Town Beach.

✪ Don a shovel and rub pointy elbows with the residents of Kununurra at the Argyle Diamond Dig (real diamonds up for grabs!) during the Ord Valley Muster in May.

✪ In July, the small Aboriginal community of Mowanjum will host the largest corroboree (traditional dance ceremony) in Western Australia open to the public as part of the Derby Boab Festival. Expect didgeridoos aplenty, dance-totem-making lessons and a good old shindig with the locals.

military-like planning to prevent you from getting stuck high and dry without fuel, food or worse – water. Yet the rewards are many; in our book, the Kimberley beats Northern Territory's Red Centre hands down.

How long this area will remain below the radar is up for debate. Last year the resources-rich Kimberley narrowly missed out on becoming the site of one of the largest natural-gas projects to be given government approval in Australian history. Explore the area now, before big business encroaches further.

LIFE-CHANGING EXPERIENCE

If cars went walkabout, the Gibb River Road is surely where they would end up. The ultimate road trip, this 660km mostly dirt highway flows like a rusty artery from Derby in the west to Kununurra in the east. Gawp at the gorge-fest en route, muster cattle with Aborigines at Home Valley (of *Australia* movie fame), and lay your head under the Milky Way at a bush camp.

RECENT FAD

The Kimberley is not the land of witchetty grubs you might imagine; far from it – the wild northwest is gaining a reputation for gourmet. Last year Rhys Badcock, long-time chef on local ecocruising vessel *Kimberley Quest II*, upped the game by being crowned Australia's first *MasterChef: The Professionals* winner.

HOT TOPIC OF THE DAY

For years the Kimberley communities have been fighting for greater protection of the region's extensive marine areas. In a recent breakthrough, the WA government committed to creating five marine parks and reserves in the region – but will it be enough to safeguard the complex underwater ecology of sharks, crocs, reefs, turtles and fish? The proposed parks only cover 5% of the state's Kimberley waters and the idea of a larger, all-encompassing 'Great Kimberley Marine Park' has been brought to the table. Now, a major government-backed research program is underway to shed some light on this watery facet of Kimberley life.

WINDJANA GORGE REFLECTED
IN A BILLABONG OF THE
LENNARD RIVER

● YORKSHIRE

NORTH AMERICA

EUROPE

ASIA

AFRICA

SOUTH AMERICA

AUSTRALIA

ANTARCTICA

'This rough-around-the-edges gentleman of the north has kicked away the walking cane'

#3

YORKSHIRE, UK

EVENTS   CULTURE   FOOD

by Lorna Parkes

- ❂ **POPULATION** 5.3 million
- ❂ **MAIN CITIES** York (capital) and Leeds
- ❂ **LANGUAGE** English
- ❂ **MAJOR INDUSTRIES** Manufacturing, retail and services
- ❂ **UNIT OF CURRENCY** British pound (£)
- ❂ **COST INDEX** Pint of ale £2.70 (US$4), hotel double per night £60-130 (US$90-200), roast beef and Yorkshire pudding £8 (US$12), flat cap £12 (US$18)

WHY GO IN 2014? RIDING ON A HIGH

If the good people of Yorkshire were proud of their heritage before, the 2012 London Olympics only served to cement what they have always thought: that their county is better than – and really the best of – all the English counties. Local athletes became heroes overnight as they helped the county clock up more medals alone than entire countries such as South Africa, Spain and even the 2016 hosts, Brazil.

As if basking in Yorkshire's glory, last year a poll revealed the North Yorkshire spa town of Harrogate was the happiest place in Britain. We're not surprised. Recently this rough-around-the-edges gentleman of the north has kicked away the walking cane. Bradford has become the world's first Unesco City of Film, fashion-thirsty Leeds has cut the ribbon on an ambitious retail development at a time when malls elsewhere in the UK are stalling, a new state-of-the-art gallery in Wakefield is giving London a run for its money, and Yorkshire now has more Michelin-starred restaurants than any other county outside London.

In 2014, this welcoming region of rugged moorlands, heritage homes and cosy pubs will be able to hold its head even higher when the Tour de France begins its *grand départ* from Leeds. With proposals to build

EARLY MORNING MIST OVER
RIBBLEHEAD VIADUCT'S 24 ARCHES,
NEAR INGLETON, YORKSHIRE DALES

Festivals & Events

✪ In May, the Saltaire Arts Trail sees exhibitions, open houses and arts and crafts stalls take over the Unesco World Heritage village of Saltaire near Bradford for a weekend.

✪ The Tour de France's *grand départ* from Leeds in July is marked with 100 events across the county.

✪ Goths from around the world will descend on North Yorkshire in early November for the Whitby Goth Weekend. Expect pointy teeth, plenty of eyeliner and the ghost of Dracula lurking in the ruins of Whitby Abbey...

a new high-speed train link that'll whip trains from the European mainland up as far as the region's cute and cobblestoned tourism posterboy, York, it's only a matter of time before this region gets the traveller attention it deserves.

LIFE-CHANGING EXPERIENCE

Yorkshire's roll-call of famous breweries (Samuel Smith, Timothy Taylor, Black Sheep) has been joined by a new wave of craft brewers (Saltaire, Ilkley Brewery and many others) – more evidence of a local obsession with real ale. So it's hardly surprising that some enthusiastic fan came up with the concept of walking holidays punctuated by

Yorkshire Triangle – its impressive venues include The Henry Moore Institute, Leeds Art Gallery and Yorkshire Sculpture Park, where art lovers can view the work of more than 200 artists in a 30-mile radius.

...WHAT'S NOT

The prospect of losing an ongoing battle to repatriate the remains of Richard of York (King Richard III) for burial in York Minster. Perished at the Battle of Bosworth in 1485, hidden in an unknown grave for more than 500 years, and exhumed from a car park in 2012 – debate is raging over where the monarch rightfully belongs. The Ministry of Justice has angered living descendants by granting burial rights to Leicester, the town where his body was discovered, rather than the county where he grew up.

LOCAL LINGO

Anyone who's read *Wuthering Heights* will have grappled to understand Yorkshire's notoriously thick accent. Things only get more indecipherable the closer you get to the Yorkshireman's epicentre: his local pub. It might go something like this: *'Ey up lass. Duz tha fancy goin' dahn t'pub? Tha's a reight bobby dazzler.'* Excuse me?

REGIONAL FLAVOURS

The little batter cake incongruously called a Yorkshire 'pudding' and famously served with roast beef and gravy is Yorkshire's biggest culinary claim to fame. Less well-known is that the region is also the heartland of British liquorice, that pies cannot be served without mushy peas, fish and chips will always be offered with a pickled onion, and crumble should always be made with rhubarb.

pubs and pints. Amble a dozen miles a day across the windswept Dales National Park, and at lunch and dinner (breakfast, if you will!) sample the county's moreish, malty liquid amber. It's exercise with a game plan; it's the ultimate pub crawl. Do it in 2014 and you might even see a cyclist or two, as the Dales form part of the Tour de France route.

WHAT'S HOT...

Ten trapezoidal blocks, housing the £35 million David Chipperfield–designed Hepworth Wakefield art gallery, have propelled Yorkshire into the international sculpture arena. After a stellar opening year, plans are afoot to become Europe's capital of sculpture. The gallery completes the

'Breathe in your spiritual self in the historic heartland of Zen Buddhism'

HOKURIKU, JAPAN

ACTIVITIES   CULTURE   FOOD

by Benedict Walker

- ✪ **POPULATION** 5.4 million
- ✪ **MAIN TOWN** Kanazawa
- ✪ **LANGUAGE** Japanese
- ✪ **UNIT OF CURRENCY** Yen (¥)
- ✪ **MAJOR INDUSTRIES** Farming, manufacturing, tourism
- ✪ **COST INDEX** Hotel per night ¥6000-30,000 (US$61-304), *onsen ryokan* per person per night ¥15,000-60,000 (US$152-607), *sashimi moriawase* for two ¥10,000 (US$102), museum entry ¥300 (US$3), *machi-nori* bike rental for 30 minutes ¥200 (US$2), seven-day Japan rail pass ¥28,300 (US$286, bought outside Japan)

WHY GO IN 2014? THE CROWDS ARE COMING...

Hokuriku, on Honshū's west coast, bordered by the Sea of Japan and the magnificent Japan Alps, comprises four prefectures saturated with culture, history and striking natural beauty: Fukui, Ishikawa, Toyama and Niigata. The city of Kanazawa is king. Once the richest in the land, it was ruled by the Maeda (one of Japan's most powerful samurai families) for almost 300 years (1583–1868). The wealthy Maeda patronised culture and the arts and left behind an array of meticulously preserved cultural attractions, fatefully spared in WWII.

Even so, Kanazawa is often overlooked by time-poor visitors who favour the more accessible sights to the east. That's all about to change. In March 2015, the first of the long-anticipated Hokuriku *shinkansen* (bullet trains) will roll into town, slashing travel times from Tokyo and giving visitor numbers a meteoric boost. Until they arrive, beds are cheap, cheerful and plentiful. The locals are ready – they've been building the infrastructure to support their return to the spotlight for years: homely backpackers, shiny new hotels epitomising functionality, and *ryokan* (traditional inns) so atmospheric you'll want to write your own memoirs – and Kanazawa is second only to Kyoto for its population of authentic working geisha.

✹✹ Festivals & Events

✪ On the first weekend in June, folks line the streets for the year's biggest festival, Hyakumangoku Matsuri, featuring a parade re-enacting Lord Maeda's arrival into Kanazawa, costumed dancing in the streets and fireworks. The best bit happens at dusk on Friday when exquisite Kaga silk lanterns are floated down the river; it's breathtakingly beautiful.

✪ Known throughout Japan, Noto's Abare 'Fire and Violence' festival (first Friday and Saturday in July), fuelled by sake and the pounding of *taiko* (drums), takes place to delight Susano-o-no-Mikoto, a destructive deity. The bolder and louder, the better it is. Colourful lanterns and portable shrines are carried through the streets with much rambunctiousness, before a dozen dudes smash them up, set them alight and throw them into the sea. A photographer's dream.

✪ During Wajima Taisai (22 to 25 August), intricately lacquered 10m-high lanterns and colourful floats are carried from four different shrines to the ocean at Wajima, with much merriment and dancing, climaxing in a seaside bonfire.

Photogenic districts radiate from the site of the former Kanazawa Castle and Kenroku-en, one of Japan's finest gardens. Edo-period streetscapes and modern architecture coexist; the 21st Century Museum of Contemporary Art is one of the most popular in Asia. It's easy to ride loop buses or rent bikes from the *machi-nori* (town ride) stations dotted about.

Rent a car and explore the dramatic scenery of the Noto Peninsula. Jagged cliffs, sandy beaches and terraced rice paddies give way to the high-altitude spectacle of the Tateyama-Kurobe Alpine Route and the sacred wilds of Mt Hakusan. Dissolve yourself in the sumptuous waters and incomparable *ryokan* of the Kaga Onsen area.

This is the year to appreciate the Maeda's foresight, artistic vision and attention to detail, before the trains start rolling in and you have to share your own *satori* (self-realisation) with everybody else.

THE VILLAGE OF
SHIRAKAWA-GO
UNDER A BLANKET
OF SNOW

LIFE-CHANGING EXPERIENCES

✪ Breathe in your spiritual self in the historic heartland of Zen Buddhism. Hokuriku boasts some of the oldest and most beautiful temples in Japan. Find them in Kanazawa's Teramachi temple district, and on the Noto Peninsula – Myōjō-ji, with its five-tiered wooden pagoda, and Sōji-ji, founded in 1321.

✪ Get some context at the wonderfully minimalist, architecturally striking DT Suzuki Museum, opened in 2011 and honouring the man who introduced Zen to the West. With its Water Mirror Garden and Contemplative Space, it's a temple in its own right.

✪ If you're ready to get serious with Zen, head to Eihei-ji in Fukui Prefecture, dating from 1244 and present home of the Sōtō sect of Zen Buddhism. Both Eihei-ji and Sōji-ji accept disciplined aspirants for residential meditation practice.

REGIONAL FLAVOURS

If fresh is best and Japan is the home of sushi, Kanazawa's Ōmichō market is up there with Tokyo's Tsukiji. Seafood lovers might find transcendence in Hokuriku's seemingly endless *izakaya* (pub-eateries). If you don't do raw, try shrimp tempura, *soba* (buckwheat noodles), apples the size of baseballs, or *jibuni* (soy-fried duck stew). Kanazawa's Higashi chaya-gai district is the perfect place to drop a few hundred bucks on an authentic *kaiseki* (multicourse haute cuisine) experience.

NORTH
AMERICA
○ **TEXAS**

EUROPE

AFRICA

SOUTH

ASIA

AUSTRALIA

ANTARCTICA

'Go hunger-busting in the haute-cuisine hubs of Houston or Dallas for a crossroads of culinary styles'

#5

TEXAS, USA

EVENTS   FOOD   FAMILY

by Luke Waterson

- ○ **POPULATION** 26.06 million (2012)
- ○ **MAIN CITIES** Austin (capital), Dallas, Houston
- ○ **LANGUAGE** English
- ○ **MAJOR INDUSTRIES** Gas/petroleum, technology, health, cattle-rearing, cotton
- ○ **UNIT OF CURRENCY** US dollar (US$)
- ○ **COST INDEX** Midrange hotel double US$150, taxi ride Dallas Fort Worth Airport–downtown Dallas US$40-60, bottle of hand-crafted beer US$3.50, one-hour horseback ride US$45, Big Bend National Park entrance per car/individual US$20/10

NEW TAKES ON
TRADITIONAL TEXAN
FLAVOURS DRAW IN
DINERS IN SAN ANTONIO

WHY GO IN 2014?
GREEN DREAM

Say *adiós* to your Stetsons and *via con dios* to your gas-guzzling pick-ups: 2014's message to y'all is that the two extremes of the Texas image – yahooing cowboy country and oil-rich business districts – aren't the only things cooking up on the multifaceted menu of Lone Star State diversions.

For starters, the long-absent scent of greenery is galvanising Texas' big cities, with Houston's Buffalo Bayou Park getting a 9.3-hectare enhancement, bedizened by hiking trails and promenades, and Fort Worth's historic heart is being shaken up with a major new plaza (bye, bustling traffic). The region's main airport, Dallas Fort Worth, will have its downtown train links completed in 2014, while Houston will open three new light-rail lines connecting major attractions.

But oh, the food... Celebrity chefs such as Stephan Pyles and Jon Bonnell have worked wonders to breathe new life into Texan tucker, and the fallout continues: fast food has gone gourmet and authentic Tex-Mex means corn from the Mexican plains for your tortillas and Chiapas beans for your coffee. The leafy, low-rise Bishop Arts District has become business-oriented Dallas' new hub for foodies and culture vultures, while cowboy capital Fort Worth is so cocksure of its culinary worth it's pioneering a food and drink festival.

What's driving this industriousness? The economy. Texas has jobs galore, and *Forbes* has included four of its cities (Houston first, plus Fort Worth, San Antonio and Austin) in America's top 20 coolest places to live.

LIFE-CHANGING EXPERIENCES

Go hunger-busting in the haute-cuisine hubs of Houston or Dallas for a crossroads of culinary styles from Mexican to Czech. Also check the state's cultural clout: Dallas' Sixth Floor Museum from where JFK got fatally shot is a shrine to the president's death and its conspiracy theories, and the Modern Art Museum of Fort Worth is among the most absorbing contemporary art collections in southern USA. Fort Worth stays true to its Wild West side, too, hosting the only twice-daily cattle drive in its Stockyards National Historic District, one-time favoured holing-up spot of Bonnie and Clyde.

But to lasso the real cowboy spirit, roam the Texas Panhandle plains and bed down at a ranch such as the Wildcatter, near Graham. Or wander one of the USA's most remote protected areas, the Big Bend National Park, a canyon-riven depression that's part of the western hemisphere's third-largest desert. And travel back to the roots of Texan-ness, the Alamo – a shrine to the Texans' last stand against a vastly outnumbering Mexican army.

WHAT'S HOT...

JFK conspiracy theories, hickory-smoked barbecued brisket, public transport, chilled craft beer at a start-up brewery

...WHAT'S NOT

Dallas (the TV series), phony Tex-Mex

Festivals & Events

○ Saddle up for the Houston Livestock Show and Rodeo (4 to 23 March), the largest such event in the world. It's kick-started by the World's Championship Bar-B-Que Contest.

○ Fort Worth jumps from cowboy to culinary on 27 to 30 March in its inaugural Food and Wine Festival.

○ America's first purpose-built (and currently only) Formula One circuit in Austin will host the US Grand Prix for the third year running in November.

HOT TOPIC OF THE DAY

Apparently, city centres can have green spaces for people to actually hang out. After decades of prioritising soulless high-rises and five-lane freeways, Texas authorities are overhauling down-in-the-dumps downtowns with ostentatious parks full of paths, picnicking spots and general pleasantness.

REGIONAL FLAVOURS

Barbecue still holds sway. Western Texas concocts a cowboy-influenced cook-up flavoured by smoky mesquite wood. Central Texans take their cue from the 19th-century seasoned but sauceless meat-cooking of European immigrants, and Southern Texans from the Mexican *barbacoa* with a leaf-wrapped cow's head starring in the grill-up. Eastern Texans prefer the traditional southern style: meat with a sweet, tomato-dowsed sauce. Despite fancy new restaurants statewide, a Texan's spiciest foodie love affair is still with a casual back-garden grillathon.

PLUNGING HOOVES,
THRASHING HORNS AND
CHURNED UP DUST: A BULL-
RIDING RODEO COWBOY
IN MESQUITE, TEXAS

'The falls themselves have many faces, and one of the highlights is the incredible variety of ways to experience them'

ASIA

AFRICA

SOUTH
AMERICA

⊙ **VICTORIA FALLS**

AUSTRALIA

ANTARCTICA

#6

VICTORIA FALLS, ZIMBABWE & ZAMBIA

ACTIVITIES   ADVENTURE   FAMILY

by Trent Holden

- ✪ **POPULATION** Vic Falls (Zimbabwe) 33,710; Livingstone (Zambia) 136,897
- ✪ **MAIN TOWNS** Vic Falls (Zimbabwe); Livingstone (Zambia)
- ✪ **LANGUAGES** English, Lozi, Shona
- ✪ **MAJOR INDUSTRY** Tourism
- ✪ **UNIT OF CURRENCY** US dollar (US$; Zimbabwe); Zambian kwacha (ZK; Zambia)
- ✪ **COST INDEX** Bottle of beer US$3, entry to Victoria Falls Zimbabwe/Zambia side US$30/20, white-water rafting half-/full day US$120/130, scenic helicopter flight 15 minutes US$140, safari from US$50

SMILES TO MATCH:
LIVINGSTONE WOMEN IN
TRADITIONAL HEADWEAR

WHY GO IN 2014? THE FALLS ARE BACK IN BUSINESS

It can't be easy being a Seventh Natural Wonder of the World. The pressure to live up to mythical expectations is always going to make it a tough gig, but there's no performance anxiety going on with the mighty Victoria Falls, evocatively known as Mosi-oa-Tunya – the 'smoke that thunders'. Providing one of Africa's most epic sights, this ain't your ordinary waterfall, as it unleashes itself with unbridled fury in a torrent of water that stretches like a curtain drawn from Zimbabwe to Zambia. Its raw power will not only blow you away visually, but the sound of its steady violent rumble and the spray that you'll breathe in and taste – and that will leave you soaked – is an all-round sensory encounter with mother nature.

Victoria Falls is shared by the tourist towns of Vic Falls (Zimbabwe side) and Livingstone (Zambia side). Leading into 2014, both were on top of their game after multibillion-dollar makeovers for their role as co-hosts of the 2013 General Assembly of the UN World Tourism Organization. Each has its own unique set of charms and points of difference.

While Zimbabwe may sound like a dicey proposition to many tourists, rest assured things are well and truly back to normal in the town of Vic Falls. Since the US dollar replaced the much-maligned Zimbabwean dollar, the economy has recovered from years of hyper-inflation, and things have calmed down politically since the power-sharing government came into place – making 2014 the best time to visit in 15 years. Meanwhile, the past decade has seen laid-back Livingstone take over the mantle as the falls' premier tourist town, with luxury riverfront resorts to match party-central backpacker digs, and some seriously good eating options in town.

And don't think Victoria Falls is all about the waterfall. While the falls bring people here in the first place, it's the excitement of a burgeoning adventure-sports scene that makes them hang around. From either side you can tame the Zambezi's kickin' grade-5 whitewater, launch yourself from the iconic Vic Falls bridge or glide across spectacular gorges like a superhero on a zipline.

LIFE-CHANGING EXPERIENCES

The falls themselves have many faces, and one of the highlights is the incredible variety of ways to experience them.

The classic viewpoint is the full-frontal panoramas from the trailheads opposite the falls, which allows you to take in its sheer force while framing it beautifully for that quintessential happy snap. But to fully grasp its greatness you're going to need to head up into the skies on a scenic chopper ride to take you over the drama. If you're lucky, you may witness the phenomenon of a double rainbow arching through the mist of the falls.

Trumping it all is the truly 'life-changing' experience of Devil's Pool. Here on Livingstone Island, Zambia, you'll find yourself in the eye of the storm as you soak in nature's ultimate infinity pool, perched right on the lip of the falls – allowing you to literally peek directly over the raging water.

RANDOM FACTS

○ Victoria Falls is the largest waterfall in the world, measured through a combination of width and height (1.7km wide and 108m high).
○ Famous explorer David Livingstone first set eyes on Mosi-oa-Tunya in 1855, viewing it from the Zambia side (now called Livingstone Island) and naming it after Queen Victoria.
○ The Big Five can be spotted in the national parks surrounding Victoria Falls – and occasionally wandering into Vic Falls town!
○ From May to June, the mist of the falls is seen from 50km away – perhaps not surprising, given there's 500 million litres of water per second plummeting over the edge.

REGIONAL FLAVOURS

Both towns are fairly touristy, but you can still sample delicious local dishes, from *braai* (barbecue) favourites of goat meat, guinea fowl with sides of *sadza* (maize porridge) and mopane caterpillars, to more international fusions such as warthog schnitzels, crocodile curries or impala burgers.

'More than a few sun-starved foreigners have come for a fortnight and stayed for a lifetime'

MALLORCA, SPAIN

ACTIVITIES | FOOD | FAMILY

by Stuart Butler

- ⚙ **POPULATION** 869,070
- ⚙ **MAIN TOWN** Palma de Mallorca
- ⚙ **LANGUAGES** Catalan, Spanish (Castilian)
- ⚙ **MAJOR INDUSTRY** Tourism
- ⚙ **UNIT OF CURRENCY** Euro (€)
- ⚙ **COST INDEX** Admission to Palma de Mallorca cathedral €6 (US$8), midrange hotel double €70-100 (US$90-130), car rental per day from €30 (US$40), three-course *menú del día* lunch from €15 (US$20)

ONCE A SMALL FISHING VILLAGE, CALA FIGUERA RETAINS ITS PRETTY HARBOUR

WHY GO IN 2014? GROWING OLD GRACEFULLY

So you think you know Mallorca because you went to Magaluf on an all-inclusive drinking binge when you were 18? Well, it's certainly true that some parts of this Spanish Mediterranean island do fall squarely into the booze-and-football-chants kind of tourism. But over the past few years Mallorca has been busy reinventing itself as somewhere altogether more genteel. The transformation has been as startling as if Keith Richards suddenly announced that he liked nothing better than a gentle Sunday-morning potter about his garden.

Of course, when an island tries to reinvent itself, it helps if it's breathtakingly beautiful, amazingly diverse and highly cultured. The energetic capital, Palma de Mallorca, is filled with art galleries and fabulous restaurants. The south and east coasts are the home of crystal white-sand beaches and shimmering blue waters that'll leave you gasping. But it's the northwest that most defies the clichés of Mallorca. Here the Serra de Tramuntana range, matted with olive groves, pine forests and ochre villages, tumbles almost sheer into a sapphire-coloured Mediterranean. It offers some of Spain's best hiking and cycling, with numerous walking trails ranging from short

LOOKING INTO POLLENSA,
AT THE TIP OF THE SERRA
DE TRAMUNTANA, FROM
THE STEPS OF THE WAY
OF THE CROSS

family-friendly strolls to a multiday trans-island traverse criss-crossing the range.

LIFE-CHANGING EXPERIENCE

When you climb up the steps of a plane in some cold, wet northern country, be warned that the beaches of Mallorca, which are licked by waters so translucent the Maldives would be jealous, might just force you to change your address. More than a few sun-starved foreigners have come for a fortnight and stayed for a lifetime.

RECENT FADS

Among the most exciting changes happening on Mallorca is the opening up of the Serra de Tramuntana to hikers. In these mountains long abandoned to shepherds, the past few years have seen a serious investment in trail maintenance and the refurbishment of *refugis* (shelters), so you can now pretty much hike from east to west across the spine of the island. Another big change is that when it comes to accommodation, quantity is out and quality is in. The old manor houses and long-neglected farms have started springing back to life as refined rural retreats.

HOT TOPIC OF THE DAY

An estimated three-quarters of Mallorquins rely on tourism for their bread and butter, and the cash spent by the masses of tourists who visit each year has done much to spare Mallorca from the economic crisis ravaging mainland Spain. But this has come at a heavy price. Large swaths of the coastline have been scarred by development, and the sheer influx of tourists has turned the island's

Festivals & Events

✪ Since 1318, Sineu has been the setting for Sa Fira, the island's largest produce and livestock market. It's held on 4 May in 2014.

✪ Over the weekend of 10 and 11 May Sóller stages Es Firó, during which the town's heroic defenders fight off Muslim pirates in mock battle.

✪ More pirate invasions take place in Pollensa during August's week-long Festes de la Patrona. The big invasion takes place on 2 August.

culture on its head. Locals want to reclaim some of what's been lost, but how best to do it without losing the income tourism brings?

MOST BIZARRE SIGHT

In a place as beautiful as this you probably wouldn't expect to find a 'Chamber of Purgatory' or the even more fearful 'Chamber of Hell'. But head to the Coves d'Artà, a cave system in the east of the island, and Hell awaits (but it's actually quite impressive).

REGIONAL FLAVOURS

The Mallorcan kitchen is one of the most revered in Spain. The local snack of bread rubbed with a garlic clove and a ripe tomato then drizzled with olive oil is called pa amb oli. Meat from Mallorca's indigenous black pigs makes sobrasada, a soft, spicy sausage used to flavour dishes. Tumbet is a layered vegetable stew. The island's wines, from the central plains, are growing in popularity.

'Here's your chance to venture into untamed territory normally well beyond your limits'

NORTH AMERICA

EUROPE

ASIA

AFRICA

SOUTH AMERICA

AUSTRALIA

WEST COAST

ANTARCTICA

#8

WEST COAST, NEW ZEALAND

ACTIVITIES   ADVENTURE   OFF-ROAD

by Sarah Bennett and Lee Slater

- **POPULATION** 32,900
- **MAIN TOWN** Greymouth
- **LANGUAGE** English
- **MAJOR INDUSTRIES** Farming, mining, tourism
- **UNIT OF CURRENCY** New Zealand dollar (NZ$)
- **COST INDEX** Whitebait sandwich NZ$7-10 (US$6-8.50), campervan site NZ$6-45 (US$5-38), half-day rafting trip NZ$130 (US$110), 20-minute glacier flight NZ$200 (US$170)

BUCKLE UP FOR A
JETBOAT RIDE ON
THE BULLER RIVER

WHY GO IN 2014? DISCOVER NEW WAYS INTO THE WILDERNESS

Hemmed in by the Tasman Sea and the Southern Alps, the South Island's remote and sparsely populated West Coast lays claim to three national parks and large tracts of three more, encompassed within a conservation estate covering nearly 90% of its land area. Pressure to exploit the region's natural resources for the likes of mining and hydro-power is met by resistance from environmentalists. Despite these distractions and funding cuts, the Department of Conservation – warden of the estate – has enhanced the lands in its care with admirable alacrity.

In 2014, the Department will open two major cycling and hiking trails in co-operation with local partners, as part of the newly established New Zealand Cycle Trail network. The Cape Foulwind seal colony can be visited on a revitalised walkway, as can the mesmerising mirror lake of Matheson and Hokitika Gorge, a hidden jewel. The Heaphy Track, the country's longest Great Walk, now boasts new huts and bridges, including the longest suspension bridge the Department has ever built. New paths deftly cut through ancient forest link the villages of Franz Josef and Fox Glaciers to their glacier trailheads. At the ghost town of Denniston, the railway and other coalmining relics have been preserved and imaginatively interpreted. Private enterprise is contributing too, with a new rainforest canopy walkway near Hokitika and a kiwi hatchery at Franz Josef.

Those who think they've seen it all should prepare for some enlivening surprises.

LIFE-CHANGING EXPERIENCES

Here's your chance to venture into untamed territory normally well beyond your limits, such as the icy faces of Fox and Franz Josef Glaciers, or beyond them into the midst of the Southern Alps on a scenic flight. Raft down the wild white waters of the Buller River, or kayak across New Zealand's largest natural lagoon and up into narrow channels overhung with strange plants and enriched with birdlife. Such close encounters with mother nature are sure to recalibrate your outlook.

WHAT'S HOT...

Exploring the backcountry by bike. The new, multiday West Coast Wilderness Trail and Old Ghost Road are just the tip of a biking iceberg that recycles the region's old railway lines, tramways, water races and pack tracks.

...WHAT'S NOT

Talking about the weather. If commenting on legendarily wet West Coast conditions, expect to hear locals proclaim that the rain falls 'mainly in big drops, and mostly at night'.

RANDOM FACTS

✪ Franz Josef's West Coast Wildlife Centre features a working kiwi hatchery, complete with a machine that delicately rotates all the eggs. It's called the Ova-Easy, of course!

✪ A great excuse for a nighttime amble, the galaxies of glowworms spotted in caves and grottos up and down the Coast aren't worms at all. They're actually the luminescent larvae of the fungus gnat.

MOST BIZARRE SIGHT

Moa were apparently hunted to extinction around AD 1400; nevertheless, keep an eye out for the huge, emu-like bird. Footprints and scat discovered on the West Coast in 1954 were rumbled as the work of a local joker who honed fake feet out of timber and refashioned sheep poop.

✪ Festivals & Events

✪ Forget the Tour de France. Real athletes can be found tackling the Coast to Coast, a world-famous epic attracting around 800 tough nuts who run-cycle-run-cycle-kayak-cycle 243km to Christchurch from near Kumara, a normally quiet West Coast town that turns into Piccadilly Circus on the February race days. It's held on 14 and 15 February in 2014.

✪ The year 2014 marks the 25th anniversary of the West Coast's biggest annual shindig, Hokitika's three-day Wildfoods Festival (starting on 8 March). A combination of live music, moonshine and crazy cuisine – such as mountain oysters, muttonbirds and huhu grubs – offers an unforgettable taste of Kiwi Country. (No, kiwis aren't on the menu – they're endangered!)

'In this otherworldly landscape, minority cultures have thrived for thousands of years'

#9

HUNAN, CHINA

ACTIVITIES   CULTURE   FOOD

by Tienlon Ho

- ⚙ **POPULATION** 66 million
- ⚙ **MAIN TOWN** Changsha
- ⚙ **LANGUAGES** Mandarin, Hunanese (Xiang dialect), a mosaic of minority languages
- ⚙ **MAJOR INDUSTRIES** Agriculture, steel, electronics
- ⚙ **UNIT OF CURRENCY** Yuan (¥)
- ⚙ **COST INDEX** Cup of milk tea ¥3 (US$0.50), dish of Mao-family-style braised pork ¥48 (US$8), plastic Mao statuette ¥60 (US$10), standard hotel double ¥170 (US$27), entrance to Wulingyuan Scenic and Historic Interest Area ¥248 (US$40)

WHY GO IN 2014? CHINA'S NEXT BIG THING

Just when it seemed like everything old would have to make room for the new in China, the government points the spotlight on Hunan. The province is a born star – scenically unparalleled and culturally rich, with remote corners still largely unseen. Until recent decades, the northwestern mountains were known only to the minority groups that called them home. Now, turning the birthplace of Mao Zedong into a destination is a Party priority and the province is flush with cash.

Hunan's cities are taking advantage of their big break. A gleaming new network of high-speed trains, superhighways and regular direct flights have put them in easy reach of every major city, domestic and abroad. The capital, Changsha, had just 40 taxis in the 1990s but is now well on its way to joining the ranks of top global cities. Both the world's new tallest skyscraper, Sky City (10m taller than Dubai's Burj Khalifa), and the first lines of the expansive Changsha Metro are due to be completed by 2014. This comfortable mix of old and new isn't what you'd expect in China, which is exactly why you should go.

LIFE-CHANGING EXPERIENCES

A journey through Hunan is as much about immersing yourself in culture as it is about

✲ Festivals & Events

✪ In February, Wulingyuan throws a tug-of-war competition to kick off the not-so-healthy eating and drinking that comes with the Spring Festival.

✪ The Dragon Boat Festival on 2 June is an excuse to eat *zongzi* (sticky rice in reed leaves), and to throw them into the Miluo River in honour of Qu Yuan, who sacrificed himself there in 278 BC.

✪ In the last week of June, celebrate the Torch Festival with the Bai people and banish bad spirits with flames.

✪ Cycling teams roll out of Changsha and into 14 other cities in the province during the seventh annual Tour de Hunan Cycling Race in October.

taking in nature. A typical afternoon might be spent perching on a low stool in a tiny Miao-run eatery, digging into some river crabs and housemade sorghum wine, followed by a jaunt into the countryside that's right out the door, past waterfalls and water buffalo to views of verdant fields and soaring peaks.

RECENT FAD
Noodle-making robots. One by the name of Ultraman is a celebrity in Changsha for its noodle-making speed (170 per minute, vs a human's 140). Robots are drawing customers and cutting labour costs – and jobs.

WHAT'S HOT...
Images of a long-haired Mao, full of youthful idealism; stinky tofu with spicy chilli sauce

...WHAT'S NOT
Images of bald Great Leap Mao, full of bad ideas; stinky tofu on public transport.

HOT TOPIC OF THE DAY
Hunan's growing popularity means not all can afford to experience their own cultural history. When the local government of Fenghuang imposed a ¥148 (US$24, free for locals and those from nearby towns) admission fee, residents erupted in protest.

MOST BIZARRE SIGHT
On the western edge of the province lies the heartland of the Dong minority. Scattered in the foothills is their spectacular wooden architecture – and a sizeable proportion of China's intercontinental ballistic missiles. The scenery is striking, but foreign tourists have been officially unwelcome as of late.

DEFINING DIFFERENCE
Among Hunan's unique splendours are the 3000 spires in Wulingyuan national park. Eons of wind and rain chiseled the distinctive quartzite formations above ground. Below, water carved out enormous limestone caves. In this otherworldly landscape, minority cultures have thrived for thousands of years.

REGIONAL FLAVOURS
Hunanese cooking is regarded as the hellfire of Chinese cuisine, a delectable mix of salty, sour, and sizzling-hot chilli in every bite. Mao's favourite, red-braised pork belly, is as common as tea. Tuck into the local flavours at street stalls or fancy hotels, and your mouth will water – for more reasons than one.

AVATAR STAR: QUARTZITE
SPIRES AT ZHANGJIAJIE
NATIONAL FOREST PARK,
WULINGYUAN

'Watch whales from the shore, snorkel among pristine coral, or just wallow in the clearest water imaginable'

HA'APAI ○

#10

HA'APAI, TONGA

ACTIVITIES   ADVENTURE   OFF-ROAD

by Craig McLachlan

- ○ **POPULATION** 8200
- ○ **MAIN TOWN** Pangai
- ○ **LANGUAGES** Tongan, English
- ○ **MAJOR INDUSTRIES** Tourism, fishing, agriculture
- ○ **UNIT OF CURRENCY** Tongan pa'anga (T$)
- ○ **COST INDEX** Beer at a bar T$6 (US$3.50), evening meal T$25 (US$14), double room at a Tongan guesthouse T$40 (US$23), room at a lodge T$200 (US$115), whale-watching tour T$250 (US$140)

WHY GO IN 2014? GET THERE BEFORE THE WORD GETS OUT

Ha'apai is our wildcard in the top 10 regions for 2014. It would be pretty hard to be much more remote than these 62 islands in the Kingdom of Tonga, way out in the middle of the South Pacific Ocean. It takes an adventurous sort just to get to Tonga, but to venture to its central island group of Ha'apai, well...

What we're talking about here is lush, reef-fringed islands, swaying palm trees, tropical sunshine, breaching humpback whales, technicolour tropical fish, scintillating sea kayaking, and even a smoking volcano – all amid a sleepy, seductive Tongan outlook on life. These are the South Pacific islands that dreams are made of, and they're virtually untouched. Sooner or later, the word is going to get out and we reckon the time to go to Ha'apai is now, before the crowds catch on.

Make no mistake, Ha'apai is not for the precious traveller. This is one of the last bastions for the truly intrepid wanderer. Forget chain hotels, boutique shopping and fancy restaurants; Ha'apai is the place to go to get away from it all. When you get there, pat yourself on the back, be like the locals and put a big grin on your face...and don't worry, be Ha'apai!

LIFE-CHANGING EXPERIENCE

There's nothing quite like swimming alongside a mother humpback whale and her calf, realising that the newborn is just as inquisitive about you as you are about it! Tonga is one of the few places in the world where you can swim with whales. Humpbacks come to Ha'apai's waters in June to give birth and raise their young before heading back to the southern oceans in October; during this five-month period you're in for a truly amazing experience. Not only can you eyeball a calf from only metres away, but you can observe acrobatic displays and hear the humpbacks 'singing' in elaborate mating rituals. If swimming next to them isn't your thing, watch from a boat or kayak close by or, if you're lucky, view them breaching from the beach.

WHAT'S HOT...

Uoleva Island boasts what must be one of the world's top beaches. Watch whales from the shore, snorkel among pristine coral, or just wallow in the clearest water imaginable. The ultimate beach-bum paradise!

...WHAT'S NOT

Overexposure. Don't be too skimpy – Tongans swim fully clothed!

RANDOM FACTS

✪ The first European to drop by Ha'apai was Abel Tasman in 1643, who landed at Nomuka and called the island Rotterdam.
✪ Captain Cook called Tonga 'the Friendly Islands' after visiting Ha'apai in 1777. We doubt he would have done so had he known of plans to kill his crew and loot his ships!

Festivals & Events

✪ Remember, you came here to get away from it all! There's not much on the calendar. The top scheduled event in Ha'apai takes places every Sunday: head to a local church and be astounded by enthusiastic singing that virtually raises the roof, fiery sermons and incredibly well-dressed locals.

✪ In 1789, the mutiny on the *Bounty* occurred off the Ha'apai island of Tofua, from where Captain Bligh embarked on his epic journey of survival.
✪ The Tongan royal family emerged out of Ha'apai in the 1830s when King George Tupou I was baptised; he later united Tonga's island groups.
✪ Jonah Lomu's family is from Ha'apai and the legendary All Black rugby player spent a fair bit of his childhood there.
✪ Ha'apai's Pilolevu Airport runway spans the width of Lifuka island; traffic on the main road is held up for planes landing.

REGIONAL FLAVOURS

The *'ota'ika* (raw fish in coconut milk) in Ha'apai is to die for! Pigs and chickens roam the streets; suckling piglets are roasted on spits over open fires, while larger pigs are cooked in *umu* (underground ovens). Tropical fruits are everywhere, and papaya is available year-round. Don't miss the opportunity if invited to a 'kava night' – kava (a relaxing concoction prepared from the roots of the kava plant) from Ha'apai's Tofua and Kao Islands is reputedly some of the best in Tonga.

SNORKELLING IN THE
CRYSTAL-CLEAR SEAS OF
THE VAVA'U ISLANDS

LONELY PLANET'S

TOP 10

CITIES

'Survey the rebeautified city from the Eiffel Tower's summit'

PARIS, FRANCE

CULTURE   FOOD   FAMILY

by Catherine Le Nevez

- ✪ **POPULATION** 2.26 million
- ✪ **FOREIGN VISITORS PER YEAR** 8.7 million
- ✪ **LANGUAGE** French
- ✪ **UNIT OF CURRENCY** Euro (€)
- ✪ **COST INDEX** Glass of wine €3-6 (US$3.90-7.90), set three-course dinner *menu* from €25-50 (US$33-65), museum admission free-€12 (US$15.80), dorm/hotel double per night €22-31/€60-350 (US$28-40/US$78-458)

WHY GO IN 2014?
URBAN RENAISSANCE

Elegant cafe terraces, majestic monuments and boulevards flanked by stately Haussmannian buildings give the impression that little changes in Paris, but right now the French capital is being reborn.

As in centuries past, much of the cityscape's rebirth is due to the shifting political landscape. Since taking office in 2001, Paris Mayor Bertrand Delanoë pushed to reduce the cars clogging one of Europe's most congested cities, particularly its Unesco World Heritage–listed riverbanks. The wheels of change turned when, in 2012, France elected its first socialist president in 17 years, François Hollande, and fellow socialist Jean-Marc Ayrault became prime minister, green-lighting Delanoë's vision. Now, 1.5km of former expressway on the Seine's Right Bank, east of the Hôtel de Ville (Town Hall), incorporates walkways and cycleways. But the pièce de résistance is the Left Bank's new 2.5km-long car-free zone between the Pont de l'Alma and the Musée d'Orsay; floating gardens on 1800 sq metres of artificial islands and pedestrian promenades breathe new life into the once traffic-choked stretch from, now linked to the water's edge by a grand staircase.

Presaging this anti-auto revolution were the Paris Plages (Paris Beaches), with palm

Festivals & Events

✪ The clay-court French Open hits up from late May to early June at Stade Roland Garros.

✪ Napoleon would be proud: on Bastille Day (14 July), Paris celebrates with a military parade along the Champs-Élysées and fighter-aircraft flyover.

✪ Paris' museums, bars and more pull an all-nighter on the first weekend of October during Nuit Blanche.

✪ During the Fête des Vendanges de Montmartre, five days of festivities follow early October's grape harvest from Paris' only inner-city vineyard.

trees, bars, sun lounges and sand lining the river each summer in lieu of vehicles. Delanoë's other traffic-reducing measures include pedestrianising and greening Place de la République, the Vélib' bike-sharing scheme, and Autolib', the world's first electric-car-sharing service.

But they're not the only changes revitalising the French capital. A gold 'flying carpet' roof crowns the interior courtyard of the Louvre's new Islamic art galleries. Nine new bells replicating the original medieval chimes ring out from Notre Dame. After years of renovations, the Musée Picasso will again display works inside a beautiful 17th-century Marais mansion. Paris' former mint, the neoclassical Monnaie de Paris, reopens with exhibitions in mid-2014, as well as triple Michelin-starred chef Guy Savoy's gastronomic restaurant and a new

brasserie. And the subterranean 1970s Forum des Halles shopping mall, which supplanted Paris' wholesale markets, is being topped by lush gardens and a rainforest-inspired glass canopy.

The world's most beautiful city is now even more beautiful.

LIFE-CHANGING EXPERIENCES

✪ Survey the rebeautified city from the Eiffel Tower's summit, and stroll from the Arc de Triomphe along the Champs-Élysées and through the Jardin des Tuileries, past ponds, fountains and carousels, to the glass-pyramid entrance to the Louvre.
✪ Paris' reputation for exceptional cuisine precedes itself, from atmospheric street-market stalls to once-in-a-lifetime-destination restaurants.

WHAT'S HOT...

✪ Wine bars attached or adjacent to experimental, market-inspired neobistros, such as Septime's new Septime La Cave in a timber-fronted former shoe-repair shop.
✪ Burgers – but not as you know them: house-baked brioche buns, homemade ketchup and hand-cut meat or perhaps truffled duck breast and foie gras.
✪ The *banlieues*. Paris' suburbs are more accessible than ever, with newly extended metro and tram lines, and open spaces such as Jardin Serge Gainsbourg flowing over the Périphérique (ring road).

...WHAT'S NOT

Driving (Autolib' Blue Cars aside).

SAVOUR THE VIEW OF THE ARC DE TRIOMPHE DU CARROUSEL FROM THE JARDIN DES TUILERIES

HOT TOPIC OF THE DAY

The 2014 mayoral elections. What's next, after Delanoë steps down? Pedestrianising the Champs-Élysées?

RANDOM FACTS

✪ Paris has the highest population density of any European capital (20,909 people per sq km), but with 478,000 trees it's also the most densely wooded.

✪ Each year there are 1479 billion trips on Paris' metro, and 110,000 Vélib' journeys per day (bicycle paths will total 700km in 2014).

✪ The Seine isn't the only waterway in town. There are also 7.6km of canals (Canal St-Martin is enchanting) and 2417km of sewers (yes, there's a sewer museum).

BEST SHOPPING

Today's hottest shopping is in the Haut Marais (the upper, ie northern, part of the already hip Marais neighbourhood). Fashion designers' *ateliers* (studios), art galleries, and vintage, accessories and homewares boutiques are exploding in this quarter, alongside pop-up exhibition spaces and shops.

CLASSIC PLACE TO STAY

Belle époque beauty the Ritz Paris also reopens its doors in 2014, after head-to-toe renovations of its rooms, bars, restaurants, gardens and prestigious Ritz Escoffier cooking school.

'Navigating through socialist Cuba's 21st-century ideological conundrum... is part of its current appeal'

○ TRINIDAD

NORTH AMERICA

SOUTH AMERICA

EUROPE

AFRICA

ASIA

AUSTRALIA

ANTARCTICA

#2

TRINIDAD, CUBA

ACTIVITIES **ADVENTURE** **CULTURE**

by Claire Boobbyer

- ○ **POPULATION** 75,000
- ○ **FOREIGN VISITORS PER YEAR** 700,000
- ○ **LANGUAGE** Spanish
- ○ **UNIT OF CURRENCY** Cuban convertible peso (CUC$; pegged to the US dollar 1:1) and Cuban peso (referred to as *moneda nacional*)
- ○ **COST INDEX** Cup of coffee CUC$1, can of beer CUC$1-1.50, cocktail CUC$3, Cuban B&B per day CUC$25, legal Cuban cigar Cohiba Robusto or Cohiba Espléndidos from CUC$8, bus ride to the beach CUC$2

WHY GO IN 2014?
DISCOVER A FASCINATING
HISTORY

Tiny Trinidad, sloping between the tropical foothills of the Escambray Mountains and the sparkling Caribbean Sea, is a sherbet-tinged, time-trapped Unesco World Heritage Site, bulging with the best of architectural and decorative wealth from the 19th century – Mudéjar ceilings, French porcelain, Italian frescos and Carrara marble floors. The year 2014 marks the 500th anniversary of the city's foundation by Spanish conquistadors with a series of fiestas and cultural events.

Trinidad is the extraordinarily beautiful result of a 19th-century sugar boom when the streets were, metaphorically speaking, paved with white gold. The saccharine revolution (which later soured) rendered the town a slumbering Sleeping Beauty. The conspicuous wealth of its sugar barons derives from the captive sweat of imported African slaves. This legacy is what provides Trinidad with a curious thrill: Afro-Cuban dance performances, African brotherhood societies and their rituals, and the hypnotic sound of the percussive clave beat – the rhythmic foundation of salsa – erupting in dance halls and sugar palaces every night.

LIFE-CHANGING EXPERIENCES

Now that private reins have taken over the state monopoly on having a good time in Cuba, experiences are more authentic, immersive, and good fun. Walk the hills with Trinidad Travels and ride through rivers with Julio Muñoz' horse-riding tours. Muñoz also does Trinidad's first street-photography tours. The state still runs dancing lessons (at Casa de la Cultura and Teatro Brunet) and controls access to beautiful tumbling waterfalls (Topes de Collantes in the Escambray Mountains), but navigating through socialist Cuba's 21st-century ideological conundrum – its dalliance with capitalism – is part of its current alluring appeal.

RECENT FAD

Most travellers pine for some barefoot relaxation – especially after a night of dancing – on Playa Ancón, a white-sand and turquoise-sea paradise 13km from town. Formerly, beach lovers travelled from Trinidad or stayed in the state-run hotels. But recently, visitors have been opting for *casas particulares* (Cuban B&Bs) at La Boca (a hot small resort), and Casilda (the old port town of Trinidad), both closer to Ancón beach than Trinidad itself.

WHAT'S HOT...

Probably one of the world's most bizarre locations for a disco, the hot and sweaty Ayala is buried in a Trinidad hillside. Dance amid the stalactites and hip-swaying Cubans.

...WHAT'S NOT

Trinidad has rather more than its fair share of the colloquially named *jineteros* (literally 'to ride a tourist'). These hustlers frequent the town luring visitors away from booked B&Bs, offering illegal cigars and generally being a fawning nuisance. Even travel-savvy folk can be tricked by these wily players.

MOST BIZARRE SIGHT

Trinidad native Jorge Muñoz has the most extraordinarily chilling collection of Santería statues in his house. One whole room is dedicated to their display; some are more than 150 years old. Knock for entrancement at Calle Simón Bolívar 302.

CLASSIC PLACE TO STAY

The super-stylish French-built Pansea Trinidad (opening in spring 2014) will be the first of its kind in Cuba. Incorporated into the remains of the hilltop 18th-century chapel of the Candelaria de La Popa, it will feature 52 suites, a pool and a restaurant.

✯✯ Festivals & Events

✪ The 500th anniversary of Trinidad will be celebrated with a variety of events from January 2014.

✪ The Good Friday religious procession of floats and followers is hypnotising (on 18 April in 2014).

✪ Each year, the feast day of Santa Bárbara on 4 December is marked with a procession and *bembe*, a drumming performance to honour the *orisha* Changó. In the Santería religion, syncretised with Roman Catholicism, Santa Bárbara's alter ego is Changó, the *orisha* saint of fire, thunder and lightning.

'See how innovation is turning things around in the disadvantaged townships'

NORTH AMERICA

EUROPE

ASIA

AFRICA

SOUTH AMERICA

AUSTRALIA

⊙ CAPE TOWN

ANTARCTICA

CAPE TOWN, SOUTH AFRICA

🏃 | ✕ | 👪
ACTIVITIES FOOD FAMILY

by Lucy Corne

- ✪ **POPULATION** 3.74 million
- ✪ **FOREIGN VISITORS PER YEAR** 1.3 million
- ✪ **LANGUAGES** English, Afrikaans, isiXhosa
- ✪ **UNIT OF CURRENCY** Rand (R)
- ✪ **COST INDEX** Bottle of local red wine from a supermarket R60 (US$6.60), pint of locally brewed craft beer R32 (US$3.50), hotel double/dorm bed per night R1200/150 (US$131/16), shared taxi ride R6 (US$0.65), surfboard hire per day R250 (US$27.40)

WHY GO IN 2014? THE MOTHER CITY GETS A DESIGNER FACELIFT

Let's face it, there's never a bad time to visit Cape Town. In recent years the city has received a deluge of accolades paying homage to its undeniable natural beauty and the array of year-round activities that take advantage of its mountain-meets-ocean terrain. This year the city is destined to get even prettier as it takes on the title of World Design Capital for 12 inspirational months. Expect sculpture-lined green spaces, sustainable projects that are more than just a pretty face, and further regeneration of former industrial districts such as Woodstock and The Fringe, now the stamping ground of hipster shoppers and gourmands in search of rustic lunches and that perfect cup of coffee.

The main goal of the design team, though, is to bridge the gap between Cape Town's disparate population, so venture on a tour out of town to see how innovation is turning things around in the disadvantaged townships, then explore suburban sights on the swanky bus system that's finally making Cape Town feasible on public transport.

LIFE-CHANGING EXPERIENCES

This year marks the 20th anniversary of South African democracy – honour it by exploring the city's history at Robben Island and the District Six Museum. Back in the present, outdoor activities prevail, whether it's a Table Mountain hike, a paddle with the Simon's Town penguins, a gourmet picnic in the Kirstenbosch National Botanical Garden or something more adventurous, such as paragliding off Lion's Head.

RECENT FAD

Artisanal edibles are big business in Cape Town right now, and the best place to sample local products is at the city's food markets. You'll find take-home goodies such as cheese, biltong, chutneys and bread on sale, but the markets are more about eating in than takeaway. Graze on bite-sized dishes mixing local produce with international flavours, and wash it all down with a pint of the Cape's Next Big Drink – locally brewed craft beer.

BEST STREET ART

Capetonian street artist Mak1one (aka Maxwell Southgate) has worked with locals to transform Substation 13, an electricity substation on the border of District Six and the Fringe which is now covered in a whimsical, colourful mural. Around the corner on Keizersgracht is Land & Liberty, a massive work by Faith47 depicting an eight-storey tall mother with a baby strapped to her back pointing up towards Lion's Head.

CLASSIC RESTAURANT EXPERIENCE

Cape Town is all about fine dining, but stuffy restaurants seem out of place in a city whose residents favour barefoot boho-chic over suit-and-tie formality. The Test Kitchen marries this laid-back character with high-end cuisine in its understated Woodstock home. Big-name chef Luke Dale-Roberts assembles edible works of art in the open kitchen, bringing splashes of colour to a dining room inspired by Woodstock's warehouse-district vibe. Each dish comes with a wine pairing.

CLASSIC PLACE TO STAY

You know a lot of thought has gone into interior design when even the air-con units look cool and the fire extinguishers exude an arty edge. From the foyer's 1970s 'object art gallery' representing 500 hours of eBay trawling, to the custom-made coffee trays in each sleek room, Villa Zest is one of the city's most beguiling boutique hotels.

✨ Festivals & Events

❂ The festival that epitomises Cape Town's year of design is Design Indaba, a long-established creative convention held in the city towards the end of February. In addition to talks by design gurus, there are music performances and a film festival.

❂ Book early for the hugely popular Cape Town International Jazz Festival, held over two days in April. Tickets always sell out, despite nearly 50 acts performing on five stages at the city's convention centre.

❂ Celebrating its 20th anniversary in December 2014 is the Mother City Queer Project, a flamboyant, gay-friendly costume party of epic proportions.

CAPE TOWN COMES TO THE
SHORES OF BANTRY BAY

'The city is reclaiming its rightful title
as the cosmopolitan cornerstone
of the Baltic'

#4

RĪGA, LATVIA

VALUE EVENTS CULTURE

by Brandon Presser

- **POPULATION** 1.1 million
- **FOREIGN VISITORS PER YEAR** 836,000
- **LANGUAGES** Latvian, Russian
- **UNIT OF CURRENCY** Lats (Ls)
- **COST INDEX** Beer 1.20Ls (US$2.25), budget hotel room 25Ls (US$46.75), two-course evening meal 10Ls (US$18.60), city transport 0.70Ls (US$1.30)

WHY GO IN 2014? EUROPE'S CULTURE CAPITAL

Sitting at the crossroads of the great empires that wrote the pages of Europe's elaborate history, Rīga was – for centuries – a strategic linchpin in the annexation of important lands, until it was smothered into obscurity when the Iron Curtain fell. Today, with two decades of freedom (and a renewed status as Latvia's capital) under its belt, the city its reclaiming its rightful title as the cosmopolitan cornerstone of the Baltic.

Over the past few years hipster-chic cafes have spread like wildfire throughout the city centre, sweaty pork-and-potato dinners have been swapped for savvy new-Nordic-inspired dishes, and hundreds of crumbling facades are being restored to their brilliant, art nouveau lustre – all in time for Rīga to earn the long-deserved honour of being named the European Capital of Culture. A generous infusion of EU funds has further protected Rīga's Unesco-protected castle core, while audacious attempts at civic, sculpture-like architecture have given the culture capital a certain 21st-century flair. A wide variety of events will also fill 2014's calendar – from celebrations of the city's German, Swedish and Russian influences to lively events unveiling many long-practiced Latvian traditions, such as folk singing and dancing.

RĪGA'S 19TH-CENTURY
ORTHODOX CATHEDRAL
WAS A PLANETARIUM
DURING THE SOVIET ERA

LIFE-CHANGING EXPERIENCE

Rīga's Blackheads' House was known for its wild parties; it was a clubhouse for unmarried merchants. On a cold Christmas Eve in 1510, a squad of bachelors, full of holiday spirit (and other spirits, so to speak), hauled a great pine tree up to their clubhouse and smothered it with flowers. At the end of the evening, they burned the tree to ground in an impressive blaze. From then on, decorating the 'Christmas Tree' became a tradition, which eventually spread across the globe (as you probably know, the burning part never really caught on). An octagonal commemorative plaque, inlaid in cobbled Rātslaukums, marks the spot where the original tree once stood; nothing's quite like gathering around at Christmas time when a majestic tree towers over the square, lights aglow.

WHAT'S HOT...

Blue cows, art nouveau, wine bars

...WHAT'S NOT

Stag parties, the nouveaux riches, vodka shots

RANDOM FACTS

✪ Dancer Mikhail Baryshnikov was born and raised in Rīga.

✪ The city has around 800 art nouveau facades.

✪ It's the only city in Europe with five different religious churches.

✪ Rīga was never a 'Latvian' city per se; it was founded by conquering Germans, became a member of the Hanseatic League, was the second-largest city in the Swedish empire, and the third-largest city in the Russian Empire.

CLASSIC RESTAURANT EXPERIENCE

Apparently, when Queen Elizabeth II spent a day in town, she had both lunch and dinner at Vincents, and other world figures have followed suit. The head chef inaugurated the Slow Food movement, and has used his restaurant to give chefs-in-training the chance to hone their craft. The dishes are of Michelin proportions, served in stylish, Van Gogh–inspired surrounds.

CLASSIC PLACE TO STAY

A classic manor house in the heart of the city gets a sleek, geodesic dome for an old-meets-new vibe; the epitome of modern Rīga. Hotel Bergs has been a cabbage farm, a turn-of-the-century shopping arcade, a printing house, Rīga's first petrol station, a casualty of Soviet neglect, and the city's premier hotel since the early 2000s. It defines the term 'luxury', from the lobby's rococo portraits and suites with monochromatic furnishings to distinguished guests including Lady Gaga.

✯ Festivals & Events

✪ Held over the summer solstice (23 and 24 June), Līgo and Jāņi are Rīga's most important days, celebrated with deep pagan undertones. Though most city dwellers flock to the countryside for bonfires, beers and naked frolicking, the capital remains lively, with parades and locals dressed in traditional garb.

✪ In mid-July, Rīga will play host to the World Choir Games – self-described as the 'Olympics of singing' – featuring singers from more than 90 countries.

'The city by the lake has become a magnet for hipsters from across Switzerland'

#5

ZÜRICH, SWITZERLAND

EVENTS | CULTURE | FOOD

by Joe Bindloss

- ⊙ **POPULATION** 394,012
- ⊙ **FOREIGN VISITORS PER YEAR** 3.2 million
- ⊙ **LANGUAGES** German, French, Italian
- ⊙ **UNIT OF CURRENCY** Swiss franc (SFr)
- ⊙ **COST INDEX** Cup of coffee Sfr3-6 (US$3.20-6.40), museum entry adult/child Sfr9-16/ free (US$9.60-17.10), restaurant main course Sfr25-50 (US$42.80-75), hotel double room Sfr150-350 (US$160.60-374.80), dorm Sfr30-60 (US$32.10-43.20)

WHY GO IN 2014? SWAP FONDUE FOR SPEED

What's hot in Zürich in 2014? Oh, just the chance to see Usain Bolt, Mo Farah and the cream of world athletics breaking another string of records. In August the city hosts the European Athletics Championships, promising some epic head-to-heads and much 'resolving of unfinished business' from the 2012 Olympics. For the first time in 60 years the event is being held in Switzerland, and locals are revelling in the opportunity to show the world that there's more to their city than bankers and melted cheese.

'But, Zürich?', we hear you say. Can a city best known for men in suits and cheques with improbable numbers of zeros really deliver a thrilling city break? We say it can. With the liberalisation of the rules governing opening hours, locals are throwing themselves into nightlife with the same enthusiasm they show for moving decimal points during the day. In the trendy Züri-West district industrial decay has given way to nocturnal hedonism, and the city by the lake has become a magnet for hipsters from across Switzerland, ensuring a Bacchanalian edge to proceedings.

By day, Zürich is more restrained, except when it comes to spending the lavish sums of money accrued on international banking deals. In addition to famous-name fashion houses and boutiques by the bucketload, the city is awash with fine-dining restaurants and bijou cafes. Zürich's reputation for living the good life has put it on the radar of wealthy Chinese travellers, who are flocking here in ever increasing numbers to wine, dine and browse for genuine Swiss watches. Join them, and see what the fuss is about.

LIFE-CHANGING EXPERIENCES

Between phenomenal feats of sporting prowess, get your cultural fix in Zürich's art galleries – old masters abound in the Kunsthaus, while contemporary shows strive to shock and surprise at the Kunsthalle Zürich, Migros Museum and the still-edgy Cabaret Voltaire. After dark, join the creatures of the night in the bars of Züri-West, or witness chefs turning traditional Swiss dishes on their heads in the city's Michelin-starred restaurants. Weather permitting, you might even get to burn off some calories with a morning swim in Lake Zürich.

RECENT FAD

Famed as a centre for academic study, Zürich has been responsible for some of Europe's more eccentric scientific advances. Among other achievements, its scientists recently perfected a way of copying lifelike human faces onto robots, and proved that people are more likely to die on their birthdays.

WHAT'S HOT...

Policemen on rollerblades, real Swiss watches, offices that are like playrooms (thanks to Google)

...WHAT'S NOT

Fondue, secret bank accounts, long holidays (the Swiss said 'no' in a referendum)

HOT TOPIC OF THE DAY

Opening the books: Zürich's famously secret-ive finance houses face pressure to reveal their billionaire depositors, thanks to the EU crackdown on corporate tax avoidance.

BEST SHOPPING

Not everyone in Zürich wears a suit. The epicentre for the city's buzzing fashion scene is Bahnhofstrasse (think Armani or Dior), but the best independent boutiques are tucked away in the cobbled lanes of Niederdorf.

PARTY ON AT
ZÜRICH'S ANNUAL
STREET PARADE

CLASSIC PLACE TO STAY

You are not obliged to arrive at Baur au Lac in a limousine, despite the Rolls-Royce Phantom in the driveway. This elegant hotel in a private park overlooking the lake has played host to royalty and served as the meeting place for Zürich's movers and shakers (the Nobel Peace Prize was allegedly invented over drinks in the lounge). It's still run by the Baur family, who laid the foundations in 1844.

Festivals & Events

✪ Embrace medieval pageantry at the Sechseläuten festival on 28 April, when local businessmen adopt period costume and set fire to a giant snowman.

✪ The biggest show in town in 2014 is the European Athletics Championships, centred on the Letzigrund Stadium from 12 to 17 August. Expect plenty of hopping, skipping, jumping and running at almost superhuman speeds.

✪ Where can you find Europe's biggest open-air rave? Why, in Zürich, of course. The annual Street Parade in mid-August features a huge convoy of 'love mobiles' (mobile sound systems) filling every corner with techno beats.

> 'If it was a cocktail, Shanghai could
> be a Manhattan, a Cosmopolitan,
> a Singapore Sling or a Pink Gin'

SHANGHAI, CHINA

EVENTS   CULTURE   FOOD

by Damian Harper

- **POPULATION** 23.5 million
- **FOREIGN VISITORS PER YEAR** 8.2 million
- **LANGUAGES** Shanghainese (Wu dialect), Mandarin
- **UNIT OF CURRENCY** Yuan (¥)
- **COST INDEX** Cup of coffee/bottle of beer/bottle of wine ¥25/35/80 (US$4/6/13), dorm ¥50-60 (US$8-10), midrange/top-end hotel double ¥200-600/¥600-1300 (US$32-97/$97-212), short taxi ride ¥14 (US$2.30), internet access per hour from ¥3 (US$0.50)

WHY GO IN 2014?
SHANGHAI'S COMING
OF AGE

The buzz about Shanghai is electric: welcome
to the city everyone wants to see (and be
seen in). If it was a cocktail, Shanghai could
be a Manhattan, a Cosmopolitan, a Singapore
Sling or a Pink Gin. Whatever your take, it'll
leave you shaken and stirred: if Shanghai's
good enough for Bond (in *Skyfall*), it's surely
good enough for you.

If China is the world's industrial motor,
Shanghai is China's high-performance
V8. The metro system – which ran to a
modest three lines in 2000 – will open the
59km-long, high-speed line 16 by 2014;
it's now the third-longest network in the
world (and for a period was the longest).
Upon completion, the twisting 121-storey
Shanghai Tower will be the tallest building
in China, the second-tallest in the world and
the jewel in the Lujiazui crown. It will house
the highest hotel in the world, a coveted
trophy Shanghai has held twice over the
past 15 years.

Beijing is only five hours away on the high-
speed train. To cap it all, Shanghai recently
expanded its visa-free transit quota to 72
hours for citizens of 45 nations, so if you're
heading on somewhere else and don't have
a Chinese visa, you can still get a three-day
look in.

❂ The Chinese New Year on 31 January welcomes in the year of the horse. People born in the year of the horse are active, extrovert, sexy and vivacious: 2014 promises to be a vintage Shanghai year.

❂ Catch the literati and rub shoulders with glitterati at the Bund-side Glamour Bar during the Shanghai International Literary Festival in March, a date for culture hounds.

❂ Petrol heads get their annual fix at the Chinese Grand Prix in Jiading (11 to 14 April), but book your hotel room up front and expect price hikes.

LIFE-CHANGING EXPERIENCES

❂ Watching neon-lit Lujiazui glowing beneath the night sky over Pudong may be a reaffirmation of what you already knew – the world's business axis has shifted east – but it's an unforgettable panorama.

❂ Discover some of the world's greatest art deco buildings, and weigh up how Shanghai goes about its business when property prices in relation to income are higher than in London, New York or Tokyo.

❂ Journeying like a bullet on the world's only commercially operating Maglev train is a one-off opportunity.

❂ Measure up how much elbow room you get in one of the most densely populated parts of the planet, and start learning some Chinese (it could take you places).

❂ If this is your first time in China, you'll find that Chinese food takes on a whole new meaning on home turf, and different cooking styles from all over the Middle Kingdom converge on Shanghai.

❂ If you pitch up in summer, witness the awesome plum rains that soak the town from tip to toe.

RECENT FADS

Goldfish tattooing – done with Chinese characters that bring good fortune.

WHAT'S HOT...

SUVs, Burberry, French wine

...WHAT'S NOT

Facebook/Twitter, Barbie

MOST BIZARRE SIGHT

If the sight of locals walking around the streets in pyjamas isn't enough, hop aboard the mind-warping Bund Sightseeing Tunnel, a hallucinogenic 647m train journey (with budget effects and garish lighting) that dips beneath the Huangpu River from the Bund to Lujiazui.

CLASSIC RESTAURANT EXPERIENCE

In a city where dining fads come and go with almost metronomic regularity, Mr & Mrs Bund stands out for being both avant-garde and an established dining fixture on the Bund. It's modern and playful, with knockout views. The mix-and-match menu has a heavy French-bistro slant, but it's not just the food you're here for: it's the post-midnight meals (discounted), the bingo nights and the wonderfully wonky atmosphere.

VANCOUVER ○

NORTH
AMERICA

EUROPE

ASIA

AFRICA

SOUTH

ANTARCTICA

'You'll never be too far from spectacular mountain vistas, rambling evergreen parks and protected sandy beaches'

VANCOUVER, CANADA

ACTIVITIES   EVENTS   FOOD

by Benedict Walker

- ✪ **POPULATION** 2.2 million
- ✪ **VISITORS PER YEAR** 3.1 million
- ✪ **LANGUAGE** English
- ✪ **UNIT OF CURRENCY** Canadian dollar (C$, on par with US$)
- ✪ **COST INDEX** Hotel per night C$80-550, ferry to Nanaimo on Vancouver Island adult/vehicle C$14.50/49, pint of microbrew C$7, Rocky Mountaineer 'sea-to-sky' train to Whistler from C$169, bike rental per day C$24, sustainable seafood dinner for two/with view C$100/200, Japadog street-stall meal from C$5

WHY GO IN 2014? FOLLOW THE LEADERS...

Vancouver delivers on nature's eye-candy – visit, and you'll never be too far from spectacular mountain vistas, rambling evergreen parks and protected sandy beaches. Inflated living costs piss off the locals but prevent urban explosion. You'll appreciate the big-city-look/small-town-vibe the moment you arrive at the airport.

From a compact footprint on the Burrard Peninsula, a hotchpotch of office towers and hastily planned condos compete for the best of some of the world's most expensive views, earning the nickname 'City of Glass'. For visitors, the upside of the condo conundrum is a sizeable inventory of hotel rooms with a view. Expect high prices during peak periods – the flexibility to visit in the spring or autumn could nab you a bargain.

People live here because they love to run, bike, swim, ski and play. Their MO is to be upfront, laid-back, forward-thinking and full of beans. So much so that they've attracted some worthy attention: after 30 years in Long Beach, in 2014 TED will relocate its trend-defining conference – attended by the who's who of what's what – to Vancouver.

Boredom is not permitted here. If you simply can't take any more of how good it gets, or it won't stop raining, or you've run outta cash, head for the hills: Cypress,

Seymour and Grouse Mountains and the world-famous Whistler (ski) and Blackcomb (snowboard) areas are within easy reach.

LIFE-CHANGING EXPERIENCE

For something completely different and a little bit magical, why not spend a night in a bubble on Vancouver Island? Literally. The truly unique adult treehouses at Free Spirit Spheres near Qualicum Bay are a ferry ride and a few hours' drive away from downtown Vancouver. Three handcrafted spheres containing a bed and cosy bare essentials are suspended from the forest canopy by an ingenious web of ropes. Guests speak of heightened awareness, re-awakened creativity and connection with nature upon emerging from an evening spent gently bobbing above the forest floor.

BEST SHOPPING

Avid shoppers burn cash in trend-bending Yaletown's design and fashion boutiques, wine bars and cafes. More modest funksters hit Main Street's thrift stores. For an immaculate collection of pre-loved threads, try Community Thrift and Vintage in Gastown.

CLASSIC DINING EXPERIENCE

We'd be doing Vancouver a disservice if we tried to pick one classic place to eat, so we won't. Suffice to say you should not leave town without exploring the sights, sounds and aromas of Granville Island Public Market. The fresh-as-it-gets produce includes wild sockeye salmon sushi, delis, bakeries and pan-cultural restaurants. A microbrewery keeps punters libated.

 Festivals & Events

✪ The up-and-coming PuSh International Performing Arts Festival (14 January to 2 February) brings people out of the cold and into the show. Gigs, galleries and performance spaces pull crowds in the name of crossing lines and pushing artistic boundaries.

✪ Guys and gals from far and wide descend upon Whistler's slopes for a week of snowy antics during the WinterPRIDE: Gay & Lesbian Ski Week (26 January to 2 February). We dare you to find a vacant hot tub.

✪ If you pass the screening process and can afford the US$7500 standard registration fee for TED 2014, you could be rubbing shoulders with pop culture's leading authorities at this 30th-anniversary event from 17 to 21 March.

CLASSIC PLACE TO STAY

Few hotels have higher reports of guest satisfaction than the Rosewood Hotel Georgia, a painstakingly restored and sumptuously furnished art-deco gem, built in 1927 and re-introduced to an adoring public in 2011. Old-world grandeur meets cleverly concealed modernity in the 156 luxurious suites – the original dimensions were doubled in the restoration, and service levels come straight from the 'good ole days'. Visitors are welcome to admire one of the world's largest private collections of Canadian art or enjoy a cocktail at Reflections seasonal alfresco bar and lounge on the 4th floor – definitely one of Vancouver's finest patios.

SKI WITHIN SIGHT OF CITY
SKYSCRAPERS AT GROUSE
MOUNTAIN, VANCOUVER

'Grab a seat on deck and look up as
skyscrapers glide by and iron bridges
arch open to lead the way'

CHICAGO,
ILLLINOIS, USA

EVENTS | CULTURE | FOOD

by Karla Zimmerman

- **POPULATION** 2.7 million
- **FOREIGN VISITORS PER YEAR** 1.4 million
- **LANGUAGE** English
- **UNIT OF CURRENCY** US dollar (US$)
- **COST INDEX** Downtown hotel room US$140-200, Blues club tickets US$10-15, large deep-dish pizza US$23, Wrigley Field bleacher seats US$50

ANISH KAPOOR'S CLOUD GATE SCULPTURE IN MILLENNIUM PARK

WHY GO IN 2014?
BALLPARK BIRTHDAY

The Windy City's cloud-scraping architecture and world-class museums take centre stage, but the real fun begins after you check off the masterpieces. Head to Wrigley Field, America's favorite baseball park, and sit in the bleachers, Old Style beer in hand, watching the woefully cursed Cubs. The ivy-walled venue celebrates its 100th birthday in 2014 with season-long festivities. Or yuck it up at The Second City, which blows out 55 candles on its cake this year. The club launched the improv comedy genre, along with the careers of Bill Murray, Stephen Colbert, Tina Fey and many more. And iO, another major improv house, opens its new theatre with twice the space for joking around.

Come summer, frets still bend at Blues Fest and guitars thrash at Lollapalooza and Pitchfork. But a couple of newcomers have cranked up the volume: Wavefront Music Festival transforms Montrose Beach into an electronic party in July, while Riot Fest brings out Humboldt Park's punk side in September.

LIFE-CHANGING
EXPERIENCES

✪ The best way to feel Chicago's steely power is on an architectural boat tour. Grab a seat on deck and look up as skyscrapers glide by and iron bridges arch open to lead the way.

✪ The Chiditarod is a Burning Man–esque version of the Iditarod (the Alaskan sled-dog race), which swaps humans for huskies and shopping carts for sleds. More than 100 teams compete in early March, picking up canned food for local pantries along the route.

✪ Every Thursday to Sunday from June to September, a mash-up of locals filters into Grant Park for SummerDance. Instructors lead lessons in samba, tango and more. Then a band arrives to play – the result is a rip-roaring, open-air disco.

✪ The inaugural Great Chicago Fire Festival in mid-October marks the 1871 disaster that torched the city. The spectacle will culminate in a parade of illuminated sculptures floating down the Chicago River.

✪ Superlative-seekers will want to get high at the Willis Tower. It's the USA's tallest building, complete with 103rd-floor Skydeck and a glass-floored ledge that'll weaken your knees as you peer straight down.

✪ Gastronomes call months in advance for reservations at Alinea, one of the world's top restaurants. The lucky ones get to fork into chef Grant Achatz's mind-bending, space-age, molecular gastronomy for 20 courses.

RANDOM FACTS

Picasso's *Untitled* sculpture in Daley Plaza wasn't always so beloved. When it went up in 1967, many locals thought it was hideous and should be torn down. One councilman demanded that the city replace it with a statue of Cubs player Ernie Banks.

✪ People tend to forget that Chicago is a beach town, with sand lining the lakefront for 42km. Some have volleyball courts and rollicking bars; others attract surfers and folks fishing for perch. All are patrolled by lifeguards from Memorial Day to Labor Day.

CLASSIC RESTAURANT EXPERIENCE

Follow the stairs beneath Michigan Avenue to the subterranean Billy Goat Tavern. *Chicago Tribune* and *Sun-Times* reporters have guzzled in the scruffy lair for decades. It's also the place that spawned the Cubs Curse. Order a burger and Schlitz, look around at the newspaper-covered walls, and you'll get the details. (In short: the tavern's owner tried to bring his pet goat to Wrigley Field in 1945. Ballpark staff refused him entry. He then hexed the team to lose forevermore.)

BEST SHOPPING

Hop on the Blue Line train to the Wicker Park neighborhood and spend the afternoon poking through hipster record stores, fashion boutiques and thrift shops along North, Milwaukee and Division streets. Quimby's shows the local spirit – the bookstore stocks zines and graphic novels and is a linchpin of Chicago's underground culture.

CLASSIC PLACE TO STAY

The Hotel Burnham sits in the landmark 1890s Reliance Building, which laid the framework for the modern skyscraper. Its superslick decor and historic pedigree woo architecture buffs. Al Capone's dentist drilled teeth in what's now room 809.

CROWDS FILL WRIGLEY FIELD
BASEBALL PARK TO CHEER ON
THE CHICAGO CUBS

'Adelaide is effortlessly chic – and like a perfectly cellared red, it's ready to be uncorked and sampled'

○ ADELAIDE

#9

ADELAIDE, AUSTRALIA

EVENTS FOOD CULTURE

by Chris Zeiher

- ✪ **POPULATION** 1.26 million
- ✪ **FOREIGN VISITORS PER YEAR** 332,000
- ✪ **LANGUAGE** English
- ✪ **UNIT OF CURRENCY** Australian dollar (A$)
- ✪ **COST INDEX** Coffee A$3.50, meal in a restaurant A$18-32, wine flight at Shaw & Smith tasting room A$15, midrange hotel double A$150-210, stubby of Vale Pale Ale A$6.5

WHY GO IN 2014? READY TO BE UNCORKED

Having always lived in the shadow of its gregarious eastern-seaboard cousins, the 'City of Churches' has been quietly loosening its pious shackles and embracing its liberal foundations. While Melbourne and Sydney have competed for attention, Adelaide has transformed itself into the perfect host city. It has accumulated some of Australia's most popular sporting and arts events, including the cultural tour de force of the Adelaide Festival, the Adelaide Fringe Festival and WOMADelaide.

The year 2014 beckons big changes for the city's heart, with the completion of the multimillion-dollar refurbishment of the Adelaide Oval, which will link central Adelaide with the Oval and its beautiful surrounding parklands, and historic North Adelaide further on. With a diversity of eating precincts, from Leigh Street – where Udaberri, a supercool Basque *pintxos* bar, draws an eclectic crowd – to the Asian-inspired Gouger Street and the Mediterranean-influenced Rundle Street, Adelaide's food scene is a delicious mix.

The local shopping haunts of Norwood and Unley have always been popular, but new boutique strips in previously off-the-radar suburbs make exploring the wider surrounds a must. Try Queen Street, Croydon, where

Industrial Revolution – a treasure trove of recycled furniture, ventriloquist dummies and '50s sci-fi ephemera – trades alongside a Scandi-inspired furniture store and the carbelicous Red Door Bakery.

A gateway to some of Australia's most accessible wine country, Adelaide is effortlessly chic – and like a perfectly cellared red, it's ready to be uncorked and sampled.

LIFE-CHANGING EXPERIENCE

A mere 20-minute drive from the city are the Adelaide Hills, a rolling patchwork of dairy farms, vineyards, market gardens and orchards. Stop for a wine flight at the Shaw & Smith tasting room and quaff the buttery smoothness of their M3 chardonnay.
Hop over the road to sample Nepenthe's sauvignon blanc before hitting Bird in Hand's cellar door for a seasonal antipasto platter and a sampling of stunning sparkling wines. If time permits, en route back to the city stop at chocolatier Haigh's factory door to complete a day of pure indulgence.

RECENT FAD

Parklets. These faux-parks scattered around the city – part garden, part bench seating – are a chance for cafe patrons and travellers to take a load off in the midst of an urban jungle.

WHAT'S HOT...

The beauty and abundance of Adelaide's beaches is one of Australia's best-kept secrets. The neighbouring Henley and Grange Beaches are perfect family-friendly examples; after a day on the sand, you can down a refreshing Vale Pale Ale and munch on some salt-and-pepper squid and chips while watching the sun set over the ocean.

...WHAT'S NOT

The rips – Adelaide beaches have some notorious and deadly ones, so paying attention to lifeguards and swimming between the flags is a must for beachgoers.

MOST UNUSUAL PLACE TO STAY

Rooms at the Majestic Minima Hotel in North Adelaide are a work of art. Australia's first self-check-in hotel recently commissioned semiprofessional South Australian artists to transform each room into a unique artistic creation; guests can now stay in rooms such as Hills Hoist or Peace.

✵ Festivals & Events

✪ Hear that spin? Every January the streets come alive with the Santos Tour Down Under, the first stop for cyclists on the UCI WorldTour. It's held from 19 to 26 January in 2014.

✪ A highlight of Adelaide's robust events calendar is the Adelaide Hills Crush Festival, a celebration of food, wine and fashion on 18-19 January.

✪ Sit down in a pop-up theatre and drink in the artistic ether of the Adelaide Festival and its cousin the Adelaide Fringe Festival, which take place annually from mid- or late February to mid-March.

> 'Food, arts and exploring the coastal hinterland are all excellent reasons to extend your stay'

NORTH AMERICA

EUROPE

ASIA

AFRICA

SOUTH AMERICA

AUSTRALIA

AUCKLAND ⊙

ANTARCTICA

AUCKLAND, NEW ZEALAND

ACTIVITIES   EVENTS   FOOD

by Brett Atkinson

- ✪ **POPULATION** 1.4 million
- ✪ **FOREIGN VISITORS PER YEAR** 1.8 million
- ✪ **LANGUAGE** English
- ✪ **UNIT OF CURRENCY** New Zealand dollar (NZ$)
- ✪ **COST INDEX** Pint of craft beer NZ$11 (US$9), entrance and tour at the Auckland Art Gallery free, return ferry to Waiheke Island NZ$36 (US$30), dorm room per night NZ$30 ($US27)

WHY GO IN 2014? CUISINE, CULTURE & COASTAL SCENERY

Auckland is often overlooked by travellers eager to head for the stellar alpine and lake landscapes further south, but food, arts and exploring the coastal hinterland are all excellent reasons to extend your stay in New Zealand's biggest and most cosmopolitan city. New restaurant areas continue to emerge, often repurposing heritage buildings and precincts, while the funky City Works Depot adds a hip edge to Auckland's culinary scene with craft beer and food-truck dining. The extensive refurbishment of the Auckland Art Gallery now includes a stunning glass-and-timber atrium, and the impressive building showcases New Zealand artists including Colin McCahon and Ralph Hotere.

Venturing outdoors, check out the Wynyard Quarter for front-row views of raffish fishing boats and ritzy super-yachts. On the city's western fringe, the Hillary Trail is a self-guided four-day hike named after legendary Kiwi mountaineer Sir Edmund Hillary. The 77km route takes in native forest and the rugged surf beaches of Auckland's west coast, and is an increasingly popular northern alternative to more renowned walking tracks elsewhere in New Zealand.

LIFE-CHANGING EXPERIENCES

Explore the islands of Auckland's maritime backyard by kayaking to Rangitoto's forested volcanic cone, or relax in Waiheke Island's vineyard restaurants. Wander along the black sands of Karekare, Piha or Bethells Beach before canyoning and abseiling down waterfalls in the Waitakere Ranges. Challenge yourself on the SkyWalk atop Auckland's Sky Tower, or zoom along Muriwai Beach on a wind-powered 'blokart'. Equally exciting is watching the Auckland Blues rugby team at Eden Park, and in 2014 New Zealand's mighty All Blacks take on traditional foes England.

RANDOM FACTS

✪ Auckland has the biggest Polynesian population of any city in the world.
✪ The city is punctuated by about 50 volcanoes, many used by the Maori as settlements and gardens for centuries. The sites' geological and cultural value may get them Unesco World Heritage status. Luckily, there's no immediate threat of an eruption.

WHAT'S HOT...

Craft beer, farmers' markets and the Breakers basketball team, 'three-peat' winners (2011 to 2013) of Australia's NBL.

...WHAT'S NOT

Traffic, and the inconsistent (but always entertaining) form of the Warriors, Auckland's National Rugby League team.

BEST SHOPPING

Auckland's best fashion designers have

Festivals & Events

✪ The Pasifika Festival in early to mid-March is a two-day celebration of food, art and culture from the South Pacific communities living in Auckland.

✪ Also in March, the annual Polyfest is the world's biggest Pacific Islands cultural festival. On six stages, school groups representing Auckland's Maori and Polynesian cultures compete for four days through music and dance.

✪ April's Auckland International Cultural Festival is a one-day event with food and music showcasing the city's rapidly diversifying cultural mosaic. Start with Turkish coffee and baklava before progressing to Ethiopian curry for lunch.

✪ Celebrating the Maori New Year, the Matariki Festival runs across a month from late June with arts and cultural performances including *kapa haka* (traditional Maori performing arts).

recently decamped from High Street to the emerging Britomart precinct. There's good eating here too, with Ortolana, Cafe Hanoi and Mexico Food & Liquor as trendsetters.

CLASSIC RESTAURANT EXPERIENCE

Restauranteur Al Brown is from Wellington, but his Depot Eatery & Oyster Bar is a true Auckland experience. Expect a buzzy, informal ambience and innovative spins on comfort food with a local, sustainable focus. Kiwi craft beers and wines complete the picture.

LONELY PLANET'S

TOP TRAVEL
LISTS

BEST VALUE DESTINATIONS

WHEN TIMES ARE TIGHT WE SUGGEST YOU TRAVEL MORE, NOT LESS – BUT PICK CAREFULLY. THIS IS WHERE YOUR WALLET WILL SMILE AT THE MEMORIES FOR YEARS TO COME.

01 GREEK ISLANDS

Greece has had a tough few years, with harsh austerity measures, soaring unemployment and demonstrations hitting the world's headlines. For a place that thrives on tourists – whether the kind that parties on sunburnt islands or hoovers up ancient culture – this is bad news. But Greece still does what it's done brilliantly for generations. What's missing are visitor numbers from previous years, and prices have come down in an attempt to woo them back. Combined with the chance to explore Greece's more popular sights with fewer visitors, this means that in 2014 it offers remarkable value. See official tourism Twitter stream @Visit Greecegr for inspiring images and links.

02 ITALY'S HEEL

If you've ever rubbed shoulders with billionaires on the Amalfi Coast or spent the weekend in Venice, you'll know that Italy can drain travel budgets. This year, look south. Italy's heel has arguably the

best beaches in the country, hilltop towns and ancient sights. But what makes Puglia, Basilicata and Calabria such good value is not just the financial side of being in this part of the country. It's the fabulous food – *cucina povera* (poor man's food), simple, tasty and cheap – and the relaxed pace of life even in peak season, coupled with good-value accommodation for all budgets.

Budget flights to Bari from Europe make travel here affordable; see www.skyscanner.net.

---

03 NICARAGUA

Costa Rica is a delight, but it's neither a secret nor really cheap. Nicaragua, though in the latter category, is fast making its name for more than simply saving a few dollars on the road. The country is an A-grade Central American attraction in itself, from brooding Volcán Concepción to the dream-like experience of floating down the Río San Juan. True budget travellers trying to make it on US$20 a day (still possible here) may think twice about visiting the Corn Islands due to the cost of flying from the mainland, but Nicaragua does offer some of the cheapest beach living (and diving) in the Caribbean.

Bring US dollars: a stack of low-value bills is an excellent resource in broke moments.

✪ BULGARIA

The days of frugal visits to Eastern Europe have passed. Especially in famous cities, costs have gone up with the crowds. This is one of the reasons to go to Bulgaria, still so puzzlingly underrated that few but travel geeks can name a city beyond the capital, Sofia – try Plovdiv or Varna. The latter is part of the Black Sea riviera that brings crowds and high prices in the summer. Elsewhere (including Sofia), transport, museums and the ubiquitous private rooms (look for 'Zimmer frei' signs) are quite reasonably priced. The most famous site, Rila Monastery, is free and offers simple rooms for pilgrims.

Whet your appetite for a visit at www.bulgariainpictures.com.

FIND THE ICONIC GREEK-ISLAND SUNSET AT SANTORINI

✪ PORTUGAL

Each year the British Post Office surveys the prices in European holiday resorts. The most recent edition names Albufeira in the Algarve as the cheapest option for a summer family holiday. The Algarve in high summer may not be everyone's cup of tea, but it shows that Portugal is great for the budget-conscious. There are excellent deals else-where too. Lisbon has wonderful coffee and sweet treats for a few euros, and you can ride cheap trams around to your heart's content. Portugal is also, for Europeans, a superb place to surf without having to fork out the airfare to the sport's traditional heartlands.

Learn about Lisbon's rattlingly wonderful trams at http://tram-lisboa.ernstkers.nl.

✪ FIJI

A South Pacific island destination on a value travel list? Yes, Fiji may just be the most affordable slice of paradise. The Yasawas and the Mamanucas are home to the unusual phenomenon of island resorts aimed at backpackers. While it's not as cheap as Southeast Asia, the value here is in bringing the South Pacific within reach of midrange travellers. Combine some island-hopping by daily catamaran with public buses around Viti Levu, Fiji's 'mainland', and get almost as much Polynesia as possible for not all of your money.

Visit Fiji Magic (www.fijilive.com/fijimagic) for details on lodgings, eating, activities and tours.

✪ MEXICO

Ignore the headlines about budget-busting resorts and savour the value of a visit to Mexico. Grab a good-value flight and try to avoid periods such US school holidays. Travellers who explore off the established trail will find Mexico hugely rewarding. North of Puerto Vallarta, laid-back beach towns such as Chacala offer guesthouse rooms for US$40, and the relaxed ambience is its own reward. Good value can be had even in the tourist heartland of the Yucatán Peninsula. Cheap bus trips to Mérida and Tulum provide all the Mayan wonders you can muster at a fraction of the cost of Cancún-based tours.

Look for *cabañas*, huts with a palm-thatched roof, most often found at beach destinations.

✪ KARNATAKA, INDIA

India still has lots to offer the budget traveller, though if you've been to Goa in high season you might doubt this. Over the European winter bargains can feel in short supply. While Goa devotees manage by travelling off-season or with package deals, it's worth considering other options. Neighbouring Karnataka's coast has serene beaches, fishing harbours and peaceful resorts, plus inland temple towns such as Hampi, one of South India's most laid-back traveller hangouts. Best of all, lodgings are cheap and most temples and ruins are free. More upmarket places to stay are opening all the time, but you'll find some rewarding budget travel here.

Karnataka Tourism (KSTDC; www.karnatakatourism.org) has lots of relevant information.

✪ PALAWAN, THE PHILIPPINES

Jungle rivers, limestone cliffs and awesome beaches – Palawan's no secret, but it certainly rewards those who visit. This mix, combined with standout attractions such as Puerto Princesa Subterranean River National Park and the Bacuit Archipelago (all available at a competitive price), makes it a great-value pick for old Asia hands and novices alike. A journey on from Palawan leads to the Calamian Islands where apparently Alex Garland saw the strip of sand that inspired *The Beach*. Watch out for the May to October monsoon: it brings heavy rain, usually in the afternoon.

✪ ETHIOPIA

While you can't get everywhere in Ethiopia on US$30 a day, you can see a huge amount of its highlights by taking great-value and time-saving flights along the country's Historic Route. This astonishing journey includes the Lake Tana monasteries and the Blue Nile Falls, the rock-hewn wonders of Lalibela and much more. True, the budget goes out the window if you hire a vehicle and driver or join an organised tour – which you need in order to get the most out of the country's wild west – but you can always save that for another visit. This is one slice of Africa that rewards the curious as well as the deep-pocketed. Budget hotels abound, but the best are newer properties – use this filter to find a bargain.

SPECIAL ANNIVERSARIES

THIS YEAR HAS A PARTICULARLY RICH CALENDAR OF ANNIVERSARIES. IF YOU'RE LOOKING FOR A TRIP DOWN MEMORY LANE, LOOK NO FURTHER.

01 THE EIFFEL TOWER TURNS 125, FRANCE

Paris' identity is so deeply entwined with the Eiffel Tower that it's hard to comprehend a time when it wasn't there. Built for the 1889 Exposition Universelle, it was only supposed to stand for 20 years. Its usefulness as a communications tower saw it preserved, and the tower remained the world's tallest man-made structure for more than 40 years. You may wonder if braving the hordes who flock here is worthwhile, but be in no doubt this feat of engineering remains both deeply impressive and hugely fun to ascend – especially if you book ahead to beat the queues.

Book tickets and get times for the tower's spectacular light shows at www.tour-eiffel.fr.

02 SHAKESPEARE'S 450TH BIRTHDAY, ITALY

Shakespeare's all about England, right? Stratford-upon-Avon, the Globe in London and all those plays about kings suggest that to find the Bard you'll do best in his home country. In fact, Italy is just as good a place for a Shakespeare tribute tour. The playwright set a third of his works here. Following their trail will take you from the sublime (Venice, home to both the eponymous merchant and Othello) to the ridiculous (Juliet's house in Verona, arguably the world's most tenuous tourist sight) via a few surprises: Padua, beautiful and largely undiscovered, and Rome, where Julius Caesar plays out.

See www.shakespeare-online.com before taking a grand tour in search of his heroes.

03 WWI CENTENARY

Chances are you have already paid your respects to the fallen of WWI. The Anzac Day service at Gallipoli in Turkey and the vast cemeteries of Flanders have long been established as essential places to get to grips with the enormous scale of this conflict. If you haven't, this year offers a poignant reason to do so (Gallipoli marks its own centenary next year). If you have, many more places to seek out WWI sights include modern-day Israel, Kilimanjaro in Tanzania and the then-German-controlled port of Qingdao in China.

A useful guide to WWI war graves around the world is at www.ww1cemeteries.com.

❂ TWENTY-FIVE YEARS SINCE THE FALL OF THE BERLIN WALL, GERMANY

One of Europe's undoubted highlights is Berlin, a city whose past quarter-century has seen unprecedented change and catapulted it into the superleague of European cities. The German capital will hog the headlines, but this anniversary is a great excuse to visit some of the other cities across former East Germany that were key in the fall of the wall, most notably Leipzig and Dresden which hosted huge demonstrations in the autumn of 1989. Of course, you won't be far from a very fine German brew to help you toast the quarter-century of the Peaceful Revolution.

The free Deutsche Bahn app can help plan any train journey in Europe, but is especially useful when travelling in Germany.

THE EIFFEL TOWER AS IT LOOKED IN 1888

☼ TWENTY YEARS OF THE CHANNEL TUNNEL

It can be hard to recall the days before the Channel Tunnel; the near day-long train-boat-train slog between London and Paris is now a distant memory. The start of Eurostar services under the English Channel in 1994 has led to many changes: Paris, Brussels, Lille and London are superbly connected and travellers can easily link previously defiantly separate countries. The English capital has become the sixth-largest Francophone city in the world. Unfortunately, you can't see fish swimming alongside the high-speed train, but minor gripes aside this is the time to sing *joyeux anniversaire* to an engineering feat that has made European travel even better.

Traverse the tunnel via Eurostar trains (euro star.com) or by car shuttle (eurotunnel.com).

☼ FIFTY YEARS SINCE THE BEATLES TOOK AMERICA BY STORM

The Fab Four first hit the USA in 1964, and neither they nor America were ever quite the same again. In fact, the Beatles visited twice that year. That first iconic trip can be traced via New York's JFK Airport and the Ed Sullivan Theater, from where they broadcast to America's largest ever TV audience. A side-trip to Miami Beach, where their second Ed Sullivan Show was filmed, is an option. Or stay in the Big Apple and visit Carnegie Hall, where they also performed, and follow the Beatles to John Lennon's Strawberry Fields Memorial in Central Park, where a meditative mosaic circles around the word 'Imagine'.

The Ed Sullivan Theater is home to the David Letterman Show. Apply for tickets up to six months in advance at www.cbs.com.

☼ THE PANAMA CANAL TURNS 100

A palindrome tells the story: 'A man, a plan, a canal – Panama!' The Panama Canal remains one of the greatest feats of engineering and one of central America's biggest tourist drawcards. It was built so ships didn't need to go around Cape Horn, and the best way to appreciate it is to get on the water. A full transit takes the best part of a day. Experience being lifted by mighty locks, passing through tropical hinterland and seeing bustling Panama City's skyline. Don't make it all you see in gloriously underrated Panama, but this centenary trip is a must.

Plan for your canal trip at www.panamainfo. com – it has tips, articles, ideas and guides.

☼ FIFTY YEARS SINCE RECORD-BREAKING SPEEDS WERE SET IN AUSTRALIA

Only one man has ever broken speed records on both land and water – British velocity enthusiast Donald Campbell, in 1964. Checking out the two scenes of his zippy record-breaking makes for an unusual Australian tour. There isn't a lot to see at Lake Eyre (Australia's largest lake – when there's water) deep in the South Australian outback, but there is a plaque marking Campbell's efforts at Level Post Bay. Access is via rough tracks and you'll need a 4WD and someone with rough camping experience. The water speed record was set at Lake Dumbleyung, three hours from Perth, Western Australia.

Good tourism websites for these trips are www.westernaustralia.com (Dumbleyung) and www.southaustralia.com (Lake Eyre).

☼ MARKING SENNA'S LAST RACE IN ITALY, 1994

Though dashing three-time Formula One world champion Ayrton Senna was killed in the 1994 San Marino Grand Prix, the race was held at the Autodromo Enzo e Dino Ferrari in Imola, Italy. Senna was not the only driver to die that weekend – Austria's Rolan Ratzenberger died the day before. Fans of Senna tend to aim for the driver's grave in his home town of São Paulo, Brazil, but hardcore fans will also visit Italy this year. Combine a visit with some of the most famous sights in Italian motorsport for a grand pilgrimage.
At www.ayrton-senna.com you can find videos, pictures and tributes to the driver.

☼ THIRTY YEARS OF VIRGIN ATLANTIC

Few would deny that the world of flying would be a duller place without Virgin Atlantic. Richard Branson's airline manages to remain deliciously anti-establishment despite years of long-haul operations. These are changing times for the airline, which launched its first domestic UK flights in 2013. Branson's mug continues to pop up around the world and he even had a cameo in the James Bond film *Casino Royale*. This year also marks the 75th anniversary of the first transatlantic flight, operated by Pan American Airways.
The independent site www.v-flyer.com helps you get good prices, plus cheeky luggage tags.

BEST FAMILY TRAVEL

THE WARMTH OF LOCALS AND CHILDREN'S SHEER JOY IN THINGS
MAKE TRAVEL WITH KIDS A BLAST, ESPECIALLY IF YOU CHOOSE
CHILD-FRIENDLY DESTINATIONS SUCH AS THESE.

01 DENMARK

Don't overlook Denmark – compact and not always cheap, but built for kids. Copenhagen is home to Tivoli, a fairy-tale of a central amusement park that dates to 1843. There's lots of free music, nightly fireworks and surprisingly good food. Legoland is outside Billund in central Jutland, with a 20-million piece Miniland of world icons (Statue of Liberty, Star Wars scenes!) made of the plastic bits (named after *leg godt,* Danish for 'play well'). The rides are mostly geared to preteens.

Stay at four-star Hotel Legoland (www. hotellegoland.dk) so you can be last on the rides at night and first in line in the morning.

02 THAILAND

Few cultures on earth will fawn over your children like the family-friendly Thai. Locals go gaga over them, and going with kids means ice-breakers from everyone from street food vendors to *túk-túk* drivers. Thailand's a great choice for an exotic trip, with temples, great food, monkeys and superb beaches. Having stopped in Bangkok with its glittering temples and fun boat trips, head to Ko Chang, an island with much family potential, including nice beaches with calm waters, easy kayak trips to islands, elephant camps in the mountainous interior, and chipping in to help abandoned animals at Koh Chang Animal Project (www. kohchanganimalproject.org).

Aladdin Dive Cruise (www.aladdindivecruise .de), on Ko Chang, runs PADI courses and offers a range of live-aboard dive safaris.

03 BELIZE

Whether you're looking for a beach to sit on, or much more (particularly as kids get past six or seven), Belize is an affordable Caribbean trip that is a boon for families. It's compact, cheap and nearly everyone speaks English. There's super wildlife to see – growler monkeys and crocodiles by land, sea turtles and (harmless) nurse sharks by mask and snorkel – plus kids can learn the drums on the beach. In the interior there's still more fun in the water, with underground rivers to tube, jungle lodges on swimming holes and Mayan ruins reached by boat.

Cabanas, often with kitchenette, cost around US$50 per night at the beach/dive centre of Placencia, a couple hours south of Belize City.

✿ KERALA, INDIA

The chaos, colour and brilliance of India makes it a thrilling choice for family travel. Elephants, palaces, castles, trains, beaches, jungles and wildlife parks are all ingredients to help keep everyone in the family happy. The intensity of travel in India could put you off taking a trip here *en famille,* but Kerala is a family-friendly version: more laid-back than other regions, greener, slower paced: even the food is less spicy and sweetened with coconut milk. There are also lots of national parks for elephant spotting, palm-fringed beaches and boat trips along the lush canals of the backwaters.

Wayanad's Tranquil Resort (www.tranquil resort.com) is a rambling plantation house with marked trails, tree houses and a pool.

✿ NEW YORK CITY, USA

There's something about NYC that makes you feel as though real life has morphed into cinematography. It's the big yellow taxis, the attitude and the iconic buildings, all recognisable from a thousand shows and hundreds of songs. This is a surprisingly stimulating place to go for kids of all ages, with its museums and art galleries, Central Park and the High Line park, hot dogs and NY pizza. This year, One World Trade

FAMILY FUN IN COPENHAGEN'S TIVOLI GARDENS

Centre (www.onewtc.com), on the site of Ground Zero, opens for business: a soaring skyscraper that visitors can climb to survey this indomitable city.

Bronx Zoo (www.bronxzoo.com) has a butterfly garden with 1000 butterflies and moths, and the Gorilla Forest's 6.5-acre habitat.

✪ HAWAII

Volcanoes, snorkelling, sea turtles, white sands, crystal seas and submarines: the only difficulty likely when holidaying on Hawaii is choosing which island to visit and where to go first. There's the steam from lava flowing into the ocean on Big Island, plus the chance to walk through the Thurston Lava Tube at Hawaii Volcanoes National Park (www.nps.gov). The marine reserve of Kahalu'u Beach Park provides calm waters for snorkelling, swimming and wading. On Maui, you can dip under water on the Atlantis Submarine (www.atlantisadventures.com) and Maui Ocean Center (www.mauioceancenter.com), while on Oahu there are the traditional villages of the Polynesian Cultural Center (www.polynesia.com).

Get snorkel equipment on Big Island at Kona Boys (www.konaboys.com); you may spot dolphins before diving under for more sea life.

✪ PRAGUE, CZECH REPUBLIC

Just because you have kids, it doesn't mean you have to kiss your city-break days goodbye. Prague is a particularly good choice for a weekend away. It's compact enough to get around easily, either walking or by tram, which is always a kid-pleasing way to travel. The architecture feels like a fairy-tale, there's a castle perched on a hill, and the atmosphere of the Old Town Square and Charles Bridge are electrifying. Take the funicular up Petrin Hill to find an observation tower and fantastic vintage hall of mirrors. Plus, if anyone's flagging and you need a handy bribe, wooden toys are on sale everywhere.

A fabulous apartment is No 46 (www.no46prague.com), with chandeliers and a glamorous feel, yet plenty of space for a family.

✪ ITALY

Italians love family, so in the Beautiful Country there's no need to ghettoise yourself at kid-oriented beach clubs. You'll get an effusive welcome all over the place and can feel relaxed in all but the most exclusive restaurants. People are used to children eating out and kids stay up late. There are breathtaking sights such as the imagination-firing ancient stadium, the Colosseum, or frozen-in-time Pompeii, under the shadow of Vesuvius. Other delights include pizza, the world's best ice-cream, beaches, boat trips, lakes, caves, mountains, and beautiful villas set in pea-green countryside where children can run, shout and play to their hearts' content.

Italians take their holidays in the baking months of July and August, when resorts are crowded but fun. Summer is also peak festival season.

✪ ICELAND

Smoking geysers, bubbling mud pots, Europe's biggest waterfalls, the ice cap Vatnajökull (the biggest glacier outside the poles), live volcanoes, thermal pools and, in winter, the magical northern lights: Iceland is a spine-tingling destination at any age. You're bound to find something to thrill the whole

family: take your pick from horse riding, elf hunting, whitewater rafting, glacier walks, caving, sea kayaking and whale watching. And, at the risk of sounding vulture-like, post-economic meltdown, Iceland's frankly more affordable as a family destination. Excellent exchange rates mean that this magical country is cheaper for foreign visitors than it has been in decades.

Flights to Iceland are affordable with Wow (www.icelandexpress.com), which offers return flights from London around £200.

☼ LAPLAND

Lapland in winter is like something sprung from a story book. Not only is this where Father Christmas actually, truly, honestly lives, but you can take sleighs pulled by dogs, ski, cheer on reindeer races on frozen lakes, go ice-fishing or snowmobile through forests. The long, polar nights from October to March offer the chance to view the stunning aurora borealis (northern lights), while in summer, you can explore the glorious national parks in endless daylight (the midnight sun brings continuous daylight from June to August) and raft down whitewater rivers.

Lomarengas (www.lomarengas.fi) has a good selection of self-catering wilderness cottages – many with their own boat to fish for your supper.

BEST HONEYMOON DESTINATIONS

THIS IS THE TIME TO SHOOT FOR THE MOON: TRAVEL FURTHER, STAY LONGER, EAT MORE AND BRING HOME A LIFETIME'S WORTH OF ROMANTIC MEMORIES.

01 CAPPADOCIA, TURKEY

The fairy chimneys of Cappadocia are spectacularly peculiar, a sight that needs to be shared. The region offers plenty of opportunities to explore on foot or by car, but the best way is to wake up before dawn for a balloon ride over the jagged landscape and fantastic dwellings. Post-afternoon-nap, climb the stairs up to Uchisar Castle to watch the sunset from the top of the area's tallest fairy chimney, where Cappadocia mingles with the clouds and everything from Mt Erciyes to the Pigeon Valley is in view.

Stay at Argos in Cappadocia, a former monastery that's been turned into the sweetest and chicest cave hotel in the area.

02 BRAZIL

With Brazil madness reaching fever pitch in 2014 for the soccer World Cup, the country is getting safer, more convenient and more appealing than ever. Copacabana and Ipanema have their charms, but the fantasy is a remote stretch of coastline where it's just you, a few locals, hammocks, and *caipirinhas*. The area around Paraty, about midway between Rio de Janeiro and São Paulo, fits the bill: remote, unpopulated and with one of the most pristine coastlines anywhere.

Pousada Picinguaba is an utterly charming 10-room *pousada* in a sleepy fishing village where the only tourists are hotel guests.

---

03 MARRAKECH, MOROCCO

Hands-down one of the most romantic cities on earth, Marrakech is redolent with Arabian spices and rose petals, lit by lanterns and soundtracked by Gwana music. The medina is virtually impossible to navigate, so it's best to accept getting lost as part of the experience, stopping for mint tea or strong coffee, bargaining in the souqs and watching snake charmers in Jemaa al Fna, the central square.

La Maison Arabe combines the seductive charms and secluded spaces of a riad with the conveniences of a full-service hotel.

✪ ST LUCIA

Rum punch, white sand, crashing waves and stunning vistas are abundant on just about any Caribbean island. What sets St Lucia apart are its lush forests, striking silhouette of the Piton mountains (a Unesco site) and adventure opportunities – sharing physical challenges and satisfactions is a great way to begin life

together. Climb the 786m Gros Piton, dive, snorkel, zipline and try the island's unique scuba-snorkel hybrid called Snuba.

Ladera, where the rooms have three walls, lies smack between the Pitons. The Paradise Ridge suites up the ante on romance and luxury.

✪ ANDALUCÍA, SPAIN

Few things are dreamier than an alfresco lunch under the sunny skies at the olive orchards of southern Spain. Think *jamón ibérico*, olives, manchego cheese and local Jerez sherry on a handwoven blanket, followed by a languorous siesta. The wild mountains outside Seville provide the perfect setting for idyllic, isolated feasts. By night see flamenco, the dance of love and passion, some of whose brightest stars – Joaquin Cortes, Miguel Rios, Rocio Jurado, Isabel Pantoja and Joaquin Sabina – hail from Andalucía.

Trasierra, a quirky hotel an hour from Seville, does delicious picnics. Corral del Rey is a boutique town hotel close to Seville's best tapas bars and flamenco clubs.

A COLOURFUL BALLOON
RIDE IN CAPPADOCIA

✪ BALI, INDONESIA

Juicy mangoes, technicolor sunsets, night-blooming jasmine: Bali is quite possibly the most seductive island on earth. This is a culture where days begin with offerings of flowers to Hindu deities at roadside temples and where every visitor is greeted with a smile, but sensual undercurrents flow. It's also the place for indulgent spa treatments, like floral baths and spice body scrubs, and of course couples' massages.

Hotel Tugu (in Canggu) is filled with art and antiques that bring back to life forgotten tales of the romance of Bali and Java.

✪ CALIFORNIA, USA

Great as tropical beaches are, they aren't for every occasion. Sometimes you want drama and power, majestic cliffs, moody fog and awesome (in the old-fashioned sense) waves. There's something undeniably romantic about a cool-weather beach, and Big Sur is as good as that gets. Beyond the sea, there are national parks with towering redwoods and plentiful hiking trails, outstanding restaurants (California cuisine lives up to the hype) and a New Age healing culture.

Post Ranch Inn is a trip-of-a-lifetime hotel, perched on cliffs 350m above the Pacific with 39 rustic-luxe cabins.

✪ COLCHAGUA VALLEY, CHILE

Off the beaten track for food and wine tourism, Chile's main grape-producing region, about two hours south of Santiago, is blissfully unpopulated and impossibly gorgeous, with the Andes' jagged snowcaps rising beyond the rolling vine-covered hills. Along with tasting world-class Carménères, Malbecs, Cabernets and Syrahs, visitors can hike, bike and ride horses (the area is home to Chile's *huaso*, or cowboys), explore colonial towns, and visit an excellent museum owned by former arms dealer Carlos Cardoen.

Casa Lapostolle is intimate and spectacular, with four large *casitas* offering to-die-for views from the baths and great food.

✪ DUNTON HOT SPRINGS, COLORADO, USA

A stay in this singular resort in remote southwestern Colorado is a chance to really escape from modern life. The owners acquired a derelict mining ghost town, gussied up the 13 homestead cottages on the site and recreated the romantic ideal of the American frontier; rugged mountains, simple living, hiking, fly-fishing, riding and taking a step back in time – but with creature comforts such as heated floors and fine linens, and staff ready to cater to every whim. New (from summer 2013) is bona fide glamping, with eight luxury tents along the river at the Cresto Ranch camp down the road from the main town.

Snow-covered winter is a magical time to visit, when the hot springs feel extra steamy and activities include dog-sledding and heli-skiing.

✪ QUEENSTOWN, NEW ZEALAND

Adrenaline is as important for bonding as the love drug oxytocin and there's no better place to get it pumping than New Zealand's South Island. Queenstown is the birthplace of bungee jumping, as well as being home to jet boating, Zorbing, paragliding and epic hiking and skiing. Many new mountain bike trails are opening in 2014. If all the activity becomes too much, there are helicopter rides over the Southern Alps to stunning Milford Sound, as well as a sophisticated food and wine scene.

Matakauri Lodge has drop-dead views of the Remarkables range and Lake Wakatipu; just outside town yet blessedly remote.

BEST ADVENTURE TRAVEL

FOR THOSE WHO LIKE THEIR TRIPS TO THRILL NOT CHILL, HERE'S OUR PICK OF THE BEST PLACES TO FEEL PUMPED IN 2014.

01 MOUNTAIN BIKING, AVORIAZ, FRANCE

Avoriaz is one of 12 interconnected resorts in the Portes du Soleil region of the French Alps, where manmade bike trails and alpine tracks create a spectacular playground for mountain bikers. The area, which includes Les Gets and Morzine, opens 25 ski lifts during the summer for riders who'd rather earn their thrills the easy way. There are more than 650km of trails in Portes du Soleil, ranging from mellow to OMG! At the end of June the Pass'Portes du Soleil mountain bike festival sees 4000 bikers descend on the region for a 75km race that is mostly downhill. The gondolas close to bikers in September, then the skiers get their turn.

The Rustine School (www.rustine.fr) offers two-wheeled tuition to children and adults. Bikes and full-face helmets are provided.

02 SAILING, CAPE HORN, CHILE

Tall ships may look like they've sailed straight out of a classic oil painting, but you don't need to set your DeLorean to 1870 to navigate the stormy seas in one, or be able to use a sextant – but you should be prepared to get stuck in on deck, and climbing the rigging is especially encouraged. The Auckland-to-Falklands route around Cape Horn is one of the gnarliest shipping channels on the planet, and you'll rack up 5400 nautical miles among some of the world's biggest waves.

You need some crewing experience for Classic Sailing's Cape Horn trip (www.classic-sailing.co.uk), though they organise shorter voyages for those with none.

03 ICE MARATHON, ANTARCTICA

Sidestep marathon sponsorship inbox fatigue by doing a race so unusual that your friends will have no choice but to sit up and take notice. The annual Ice Marathon takes place in temperatures of -20°C though the brutal wind chill whipping round your chops can make it feel another 20 degrees below that. It's an environment so hostile even penguins won't call it home. Yet to marathon in this frosted world you don't actually need prior experience of running in extreme cold. You do need to follow advice on what to wear as if your life depends on it, as it probably does.

The 2014 Ice Marathon (www.icemarathon.com) is set for 19 to 23 November but the dates depend on the weather.

✿ SWIMMING, SPORADES ISLES, GREECE

You don't have to watch *The Beach* to figure out that swimming from one island to another is a pretty magical way to arrive at your holiday destination. In this tour of a superquiet stretch of the Aegean Sea you get to do that every day, Greek island–hopping stroke by stroke without the bother of carrying your kit, which will follow behind in the support boat. You'll be sharing the craggy coastlines of the Sporades archipelago and its protected turquoise waters with dolphins, seals and scientists, as the area is part of Europe's largest natural marine park.

Swim Trek (www.swimtrek.com) runs trips in June and July with average daily swims of 5km. Video analysis is on offer to help hone your stroke technique.

✿ CLIMBING MOUNT BAKER ON SNOWBOARD OR SKIS, WASHINGTON, USA

Scaling a summit, though always impressive, is a lot more fun if you plan to reward yourself with a hefty dose of adrenaline on the way down, rather than an energy depleted trudge back to base. It's also a lot easier and faster to climb using skis instead of feet and now snowboarders can join the party by using splitboards. The peak of Mount Baker is 3285m and on the ascent, which includes glacial terrain, you'll have stunning panoramic

THE THRILL AND SPILLS OF MOUNTAIN BIKING IN THE PORTES DU SOLEIL

Alpine views plus the sight of the San Juan Islands and Washington's inland waters to distract you from your toil.

The American Alpine Institute (www.alpine institute.com) runs three-day trips in May and June; you'll need intermediate touring and riding experience to get involved.

☼ KAYAKING, KAMCHATKA, RUSSIA

For an experience so edge-of-the-world you'll need to be careful you don't actually drop off, this 160km hike and kayak expedition in remotest Kamchatka takes some beating. Your small group will be dropped by helicopter at the foot of the Karimsky volcano, where you'll begin crossing the Siberian taiga. You'll encounter no roads or people, the only tracks being those of the 25,000 brown bears who call this region home. When you reach the headwaters of the salmon- and trout-rich Zhupanova river, you'll take to your kayak and paddle its entire length to the Bering Sea.

For this Natural Habitat Expedition (www. nathab.com), done in partnership with WWF, you'll need multiday paddling experience in rivers and oceans.

☼ ROCK CLIMBING, YANGSHUO, CHINA

Yangshuo, a picturesque former fishing village, has found itself dubbed the adventure capital of China thanks in part to its accessibility but mostly due to the rock-climbing opportunities afforded by its many limestone karst peaks, which rise strikingly from the dense emerald-green vegetation. A buzzing scene of local and international climbers enjoy arguably the best concentration of climbs in Asia, most of which are reachable by a short bike or bus ride from downtown. Many routes are well bolted, though the more intrepid climber can still find fresh, and in some cases near-vertical, routes to conquer.

Insight Adventures (www.insight-adventures. com) do trips to Yangshuo. The best times are March to May and September to December; there's a climbing festival in November.

☼ STAND-UP PADDLE-BOARDING, DOMINICAN REPUBLIC

If you plan on stand-up paddling (SUP), you'll want to seek out spots that remain relatively empty, rather than popular surf breaks which increasingly resemble the scrums that follow door-opening at the January sales. The rugged northern coastline of the Dominican Republic offers 500km of such bounty buffeted by North Atlantic swells, and SUP is an easy way to catch these waves, while giving you the option of exploring the region's river mouths, outer reefs and crystal-blue Caribbean coves in a manner so civilised you may not even need to get your swimmers wet.

Waterways Travel (www.waterwaystravel. com) runs tours most of the year but May to September is the best time to visit for small, fun waves with zero crowds.

☼ WHITEWATER RAFTING, MOSQUITO COAST, HONDURAS

The swamp-ridden jungle that makes up the Mosquito Coast, named after the local Miskito Indians rather than the pesky blood-suckers, is one of the least explored areas in the Americas. Yet the truly hardy can whitewater raft through its core, riding the Rio

**EXPECT TO GET WET
WHITEWATER RAFTING
IN HONDURAS**

Platano river to the Caribbean coast with only the region's indigenous tribes and unique wildlife (river otters, scarlet macaws, pumas, jaguars and vampire bats) for company. When not riding the rapids, you'll explore the caves and subterranean creeks (once used for ancient rituals) that line the river, and by night you'll hone your bushcraft skills by wild camping on the sandy riverbanks.
Epic Tomato (epictomato.com) organises the week-long rafting trips, after which it will transport you to a hidden coastal retreat to snorkel and rest.

☼ TRAVEL BY HORSE AND CART, MYANMAR

Exploring the ruins of the ancient city Ava by horse and cart is not a tourist gimmick but simply the only way to get around. It's also the best way to see the Buddhist temples and pagodas in Bagan. Still a popular mode of transport for locals, especially in rural areas, it's not the smoothest ride nor the speediest, but at least that means you can enjoy your view rather than have everything flying past in one big whoosh. You'll be sheltered from the sun and rain, should either get too full-on.
All Points East (allpointseast.com) runs tours of Myanmar. Alongside horse and cart, transport options include bike, local train, rickshaw and Irrawaddy cruiser.

BEST BEACHES & SMALL ISLANDS

2014 IS THE INTERNATIONAL YEAR OF SMALL ISLAND DEVELOPING STATES: TINY, REMOTE AND ENVIRONMENTALLY VULNERABLE SPOTS. HERE ARE 10 THAT NEED YOU – AND ARE GLORIOUS TOO!

01 PALAU

The Micronesian nation of Palau isn't formed so much of islands as giant green mushrooms. Certainly that's how its Rock Archipelago appears: a bloom of over 200 lush limestone islets undercut by azure seas and fringed by sugary sand. It's ideal kayaking territory, though if you tire of paddling, you can always flop overboard to float above some of the world's best subaqua action (according to famed diver Jacques Cousteau). For added weirdness, save your snorkel for Jellyfish Lake, where millions of gelatinous zooplankton – which have lost the ability to sting – perform a benignly beautiful underwater ballet.

Palau International Airport, on Babeldaob island, has flights from Taipei (4hr 55min), Guam (1hr 45min) and Manila (2hr 35min).

02 TONGA

Tonga is not your common or garden paradise. Yes, its 170-odd isles are idyllically sprinkled across the bluest South Pacific; its flawless sands are tickled by palms and want-to-dive-into seas. But it's also the region's only remaining kingdom, where globalisation has yet to entirely erode its Polynesian traditions: locals still weave mats, wear *tupenu* skirts and gossip over intoxicating kava. Ha'apai is the place for empty beaches and super snorkelling; Niuas is even more perfect and remote. Vava'u is preferred by the South Pacific's humpbacks – each year, these whales come here to breed, and travellers come to jump in with them.

Humpbacks migrate to Tonga from around early July to late October; strict guidelines apply to swimming and watching the whales.

03 SÃO TOMÉ & PRÍNCIPE

Middle of the world but not middle of the road, the equator-hovering outcrops of São Tomé and Príncipe form Africa's smallest, and perhaps least-known, state. Part of a chain of extinct volcanoes, they hide in the Gulf of Guinea, west of Gabon, which explains why so few tourists manage to find them. Those that do are richly rewarded, though: there are miles of sandy beaches trodden only by fishermen; a jungly interior with a 2024m peak to

climb; turtles and humpbacks splashing
in the waters; and hotels set in crumbly
colonial plantation houses, which offer an
atmospheric cool-breezed base.

The dry season is June to September, wet is
from October to May; humpbacks visit the
waters off São Tomé from July to October.

☼ TRINIDAD & TOBAGO

Bountiful birds, steel-pan bands, street
food, rainforest, multiculture and a raucous
Carnival – that's what Trinidad's made of.
This is the Caribbean at its most exhilarating,
least contrived and, strangely, most beach-
free. There are nice strands, but Trinidad isn't
about lolling in paradise: it's about living it.

Besides, sister-isle Tobago fills all the basic
sand-nirvana needs. Its west is edged with
unspoiled palmy shores, where tourism
remains low-key. Its east, however, is that bit
wilder: South American–style flora blooms
in abundance; caiman and other critters lurk
in the forest; and the coast is notched with
secret coves, perfect for that castaway feel.

Dry season is December to May, wet is June
to November. The islands sit just outside the
hurricane belt (hurricanes do occur at times).

☼ COOK ISLANDS

Captain Cook would be proud. The 15-island
archipelago that bears the explorer's name
is a beaut, incorporating some of the South

Pacific's best sand-palm-sea paradises (it's impossible not to drool into Aitutaki's cerulean lagoon). Better still, it's accessible. Of course, when you're talking specks in an 165-million-sq-km ocean, accessibility is relative. But with many an Oz-to-USA flight touching down on the main island, Rarotonga, visiting the Cooks isn't just a pipe dream. Be warned, though: those that do stop-off – to hike through jungle, kayak to a private atoll or do nothing much at all – find it hard to leave. Seasonal weather variations are slight: temperatures are from 18°C to 28°C May to October or 21°C to 29°C November to April.

☼ PAPUA NEW GUINEA

PNG is about the size of California. But within its broiling, savage and spectacular confines you'll find, for example, more than 190 species of mammals, 650 species of (often bonkers) birds, 160 types of frogs and 820 different languages. Simply, it's one of the wildest, most megadiverse and most singular places on the planet. For tribal encounters, head to the Highlands (to Tari to meet the Wigmen, to Mt Hagen for its festival). But don't ignore the coast, where reef walls drop to inky depths just metres from magnificent beaches to provide some of the best diving and snorkelling in the world. Transport in PNG is challenging; its few roads are in poor condition. Internal flights and tours are the easiest ways to travel.

☼ CAPE VERDE

First colonised by the Portuguese, geographically closest to West Africa and with a Latin vibe that feels a bit like Brazil, the Cape Verde archipelago is hard to pigeonhole. It's pretty hard to place on a map, too, lurking some

500km off the coast of Senegal amid a whole lot of Atlantic Ocean. There are 10 islands, from lava-streaked Fogo to the luxuriant valleys of Santo Antão. But the best beaches belong to Boa Vista, an island virtually subsumed by sand: Sahara-style dunes ripple the interior, while miles of gorgeous graininess edge the breezy shores, perfect for windsurfing off into the blue beyond. Boa Vista is an important nesting site for loggerhead turtles; the best time to see them is June to September.

☼ GRENADA

You could come to the Caribbean's lush-n-lovely Spice Island, plonk down on Grand Anse (its 3km-long beach) and be more than satisfied: the sand's fine, the beach bars lively, the restaurants well stocked with seafood and nutmeg ice cream. But that would be a waste, for the mountainous innards of this Windward Isle have created coves and inlets ideal for secluded swims and snorkels. Even more intimate and a ferry-hop west is Carriacou, with wild sands only reached by hiking or sailing, and a thriving African culture that ensures a soundtrack of big drums and captivating calypso. Up to three flights a day link Grenada and Carriacou; a crossing by ferry takes from 90 minutes.

☼ SEYCHELLES

Nary a 'world's best beach' list is compiled without the Seychelles getting a mention. This clutch of 115 islands sprinkled in the Indian Ocean got all the good genes: its waters are clear and teeming with life; its sands are sensuously soft; its interiors are wild and luscious; even its coconuts – the

buttocky coco-de-mer – are sort of sexy. The three main islands (Praslin, Mahé and La Digue) are perfectly pretty. Even better are Curieuse, where giant tortoises lumber, and the coral atoll of Aldabra, uninhabited but for more tortoises (the world's largest population), plus turtles, sharks, coconut crabs and a wealth of species besides.

Seychelles International Airport is 8km south of Victoria, on Mahé. Regular ferry services run between Praslin, Mahé and La Digue.

ST VINCENT & THE GRENADINES

Know your budget, choose your boat – that's the key to unlocking this lovely island chain in the southeast Caribbean. If your wallet's well-endowed, travel by private yacht, from large, green and gorgeous St Vincent down the tail of the unblemished Grenadines – small specks, big on charm. Those without an oligarch's income should hop by fun ferries. Join the locals (and their luggage/mail/chickens) making their way from St Vincent to Bequia's lively waterfront, the fine sands of Canouan, rugged Union and languid Mayreau; from here, the deserted Tobago Cays (where one Jack Sparrow was once cast away) beckon beautifully just to the east.

The MV Barracuda and MV Gem Star ferries operate regular services between Kingstown (St Vincent) and the southern Grenadines.

100 YEARS SINCE THE FIRST WORLD WAR

THIS YEAR MARKS THE CENTENARY OF THE START OF THE GREAT WAR (28 JULY 1914 TO 11 NOVEMBER 1918). HERE ARE SOME POIGNANT REMINDERS OF THIS DEVASTATING CONFLICT.

01 POPPY FIELDS, FLANDERS, BELGIUM

'In Flanders fields the poppies grow; between the crosses, row on row...' Probably the most celebrated of the WWI poems, these beautifully evocative opening lines were penned by a Canadian Lieutenant Colonel, John McCrae, in homage to a lost friend. As war ravaged the countryside and churned the earth, the disturbance stimulated the growth of poppies; they illuminated the countryside and have since become the defining image of remembrance to the dead. The poppies still bloom each year, providing nature's own homage to the bravery of those who made the greatest sacrifice.

Poppies are in bloom on the Western Front battlefields from April to early July, but unseasonal weather can affect their growth.

02 GALLIPOLI, TURKEY

Away from northern Europe's front lines, some of the fiercest fighting occurred at Gallipoli. This eight-month campaign proved disastrous for Allied forces – some 34,000 Brits, Aussies and Kiwis perished here. The Gallipoli peninsula is 240km southwest of İstanbul, flanked by the Aegean Sea on one side and the Dardanelles channel on the other. The Allied plan was simple – send a flotilla up the Dardanelles to seize control of İstanbul and open a naval passage to Russia. But Ottoman troops provided unflinching resistance that forced the Allies to withdraw. Trooper Tours (www.troopertours.com) will take you around the key sites in Gallipoli.

---

03 TYNE COT CEMETERY, ZONNEBEKE, BELGIUM

Of all the Commonwealth cemeteries marking the fallen heroes of WWI, Tyne Cot is the largest, containing 11,954 graves of soldiers from the UK, Canada, Australia, New Zealand, South Africa and the West Indies. The cemetery also carries the names of a further 35,000 soldiers who were never found. At the centre of the graves, the Commonwealth Cross of Sacrifice stands atop a German pillbox, overlooking row upon row of white headstones. There's no more powerful introduction to the sorrow of war. Zonnebeke is 75km south of Bruges. Combine a visit to Tyne Cot with a trip to the Memorial Museum Passchendaele 1917 (www.passchendaele.be).

☼ CHRISTMAS TRUCE MEMORIAL, FRELINGHIEN, FRANCE

Amid the horror of front-line fighting, stories of simple humanity have become legend; none more so than the Christmas Truce of 1914. With the war still in its infancy, hundreds of Allied and German soldiers near the French town of Frelinghien downed their guns on Christmas Day and engaged in a remarkable truce. Official records are sketchy but the most famous story recollects a football

FLANDERS' FIELDS ARE RED WITH POPPIES; REMEMBRANCE DAY IS IN NOVEMBER

match on the battlefield – nobody has been able to corroborate this, but enough evidence of the truce exists for it to be marked with a plaque at the edge of the village.

Frelinghien is 90km southwest of Calais; combine it with a visit to Ieper, 15km north.

❂ MENIN GATE MEMORIAL, IEPER, BELGIUM

The battlefields around Ypres saw appalling conflict. At the eastern end of town stands Menin Gate, a memorial to more than 54,000 soldiers whose final resting place remains unknown. Every evening at 8pm, the road beneath the arch is closed to traffic and buglers from the local fire brigade sound the Last Post, the haunting commemoration to soldiers lost in war. On summer evenings the event draws large crowds who stand silent in remembrance; in the bleak winter, the bugle notes drift away in the wind.

Ypres is now known by its Flemish name, Ieper. Menin Gate is close to the marketplace.

❂ WILFRED OWEN'S GRAVE, ORS, FRANCE

Wilfred Owen was a British poet and one of WWI's most celebrated voices. He enlisted in October 1915, and his work was influenced both by battlefield trauma and the writing of his friend, Siegfried Sassoon. His poems are regarded as the finest records of first-hand experience – *Anthem for Doomed Youth* is among the most famous. Owen was killed one week before Armistice Day – the telegram informing his mother was delivered amid victory celebrations – and his grave can be found in the Ors Communal Cemetery.

The village of Ors lies between Le Cateau and Landrecies, 85km southeast of Lille.

❂ LATIN BRIDGE, SARAJEVO, BOSNIA & HERCEGOVINA

When Archduke Franz Ferdinand of Austria was assassinated in Sarajevo on 28 June 1914, few would have imagined the carnage that would follow. Ferdinand was targeted by a revolutionary movement known as Young Bosnia, and his death was the catalyst that led Austria-Hungary to declare war on Serbia. Germany, allied to Austria-Hungary, soon joined the fold. The spot of Ferdinand's death was close to the Latin Bridge in the heart of the city, and a small plaque commemorates the event. There's no fuss and precious little pomp, but for budding historians a visit here forms part of the ultimate WWI pilgrimage.

Sarajevo is one of Europe's up-and-coming cities, so you can combine your history fix with top shopping and entertainment.

❂ ARMISTICE GLADE, RETHONDES, FRANCE

11 November 1918; the end of the Great War. After four long years, and with Europe on its knees, Germany accepted the armistice conditions proposed by the Allies. Under the command of Marshal Ferdinand Foch of the French Army, the selected congressmen assembled to sign the treaty. The location Foch chose was the carriage of his personal train, secluded in the tranquil forest of Compiègne. Today the forest hides a glade with a war memorial, under the gaze of Foch's statue. Alongside lies a reconstruction of the Armistice Carriage – the original was seized by Nazi troops in WWII and destroyed in 1945.

The Armistice Glade lies between Rethondes and Compiègne (route D546). Trains (www. sncf.com) run from Paris Nord to Compiègne.

☼ TRENCH OF DEATH, DIKSMUIDE, BELGIUM

The Western Front was a trench network covering thousands of kilometres, extending south from Nieuwpoort on the Belgian coast to the French border with Switzerland. Bitterly cold, waterlogged and thick with mud, the trenches offered soldiers precious little protection. In the countryside, 1.5km from the town of Diksmuide, a small section has been preserved. Known as the 'Trench of Death', conservation work ensures that this remains a unique example of battlefield life. The Trench of Death is 45km southwest of Bruges, which makes a good base for exploring other battlefields and cemeteries.

☼ LOCHNAGAR CRATER, LA BOISSELLE, FRANCE

The five-month-long Battle of the Somme was one of WWI's defining battles, with more than a million dead. Yet few know that its roots lay deep beneath the battlefield. In an attempt to outfox the Germans, British troops started the offensive by blowing them up from below. Tunnelling teams laid 10 huge mines under enemy lines, detonating them simultaneously. Stuffed with 28.8 tonnes of explosives, the assault gave the Allies an advantage in the battle. The massive crater (90m across, 30m deep) can still be seen. La Boisselle is 155km north of Paris. From the village, follow the signs for 'La Grande Mine'.

BEST BEATLEMANIA

IT'S 50 YEARS SINCE THE BEATLES LANDED IN NEW YORK IN 1964, CHANGING POP MUSIC FOREVER. HERE'S A MAGICAL MYSTERY TOUR WITH THE FAB FOUR.

01 REEPERBAHN, HAMBURG, GERMANY

John Lennon once said, 'I might have been born in Liverpool but I grew up in Hamburg.' This raunchy city was so instrumental to the early Beatles that a plaza in the St Pauli district was named 'Beatles-Platz' in 2006. The plaza, paved black to resemble a vinyl record, is in the heart of the Reeperbahn, a street known for its nightlife and Hamburg's red-light district. From 1960 to 1962, the leather-clad Fab Five (including original bassist Stuart Sutcliffe) played hundreds of gigs in this naughty neighbourhood, though most of the clubs have closed down.
The Indra Musik Club (www.indramusikclub.com), site of the first Beatles gig in Hamburg, still hosts live music.

02 CAVERN CLUB, LIVERPOOL, ENGLAND

No-one could have guessed that four working-class lads from Liverpool would become bigger than Elvis. But Ob-La-Di, Ob-La-Da, it happened. The earliest sounds of Beatlemania could be heard at the Cavern Club (www.cavernclub.org), a tiny live music venue that is still open today and has also hosted bands like the Who, Oasis and the Arctic Monkeys. For fans searching for the Beatles' roots – all you need is Liverpool. From Penny Lane to the former Strawberry Fields children's home behind John Lennon's aunt Mimi's house, the city is a living, breathing Beatles museum.
The Beatles Story Museum (www.beatlesstory.com) features a replica of the Cavern Club and a Fab 4D animated cinema show.

03 STRAWBERRY FIELDS, NEW YORK CITY, USA

A simple memorial garden that has become a global symbol of peace, Strawberry Fields is one of the most tranquil corners of Central Park. Founded on 9 October 1985, the 45th anniversary of Lennon's birth, near the Dakota Building where he was killed, the garden was designed by Yoko Ono and architect Bruce Kelly. The black-and-white meditative mosaic made by Italian craftsmen revolves around one word: 'Imagine'. Lennon, who Ono said was born a New Yorker,

THE MOSAIC IN
CENTRAL PARK'S
STRAWBERRY
FIELDS

moved to the Big Apple in 1971, first living in Greenwich Village, and even recorded an album called *Sometime in New York City*. Lennon's only full-length solo concert was played at Madison Square Garden (www. thegarden.com), which hosts NBA games and big-name music acts.

☼ PARADISE ISLAND, THE BAHAMAS

Following the success of their first film *A Hard Day's Night*, Beatles director Richard Lester had a bigger budget for *Help!* Cheekily, the Beatles requested the Bahamas as a location simply because they hadn't been there, so in February 1965

they arrived in the city of Nassau on New Providence Island, connected to Paradise Island by a bridge. However, the band didn't have a single day off on Paradise Island, which also features in the James Bond films *Casino Royale* and *Thunderball*. Paradise Island is now home to Vegas-style casino resorts and the Aquaventure Waterpark, with its mammoth Mayan Temple waterslide. For information on hotel resorts and night-clubs, as well as diving and watersports, see www.nassauparadiseisland.com.

☼ RISHIKESH, INDIA

After the Beatles met a giggling guru called the Maharishi (meaning 'enlightened spiritual one') in London in August 1967, they were eager to 'turn off their minds' with more transcendental meditation. So in February 1968 they joined Donovan, Mia Farrow and Mike Love from the Beach Boys at the Maharishi's ashram, located in the Valley of the Saints on the River Ganges in the foothills of the Himalayas. The Beatles stayed for six weeks and wrote much of *The White Album* here. Rishikesh is now considered the yoga capital of the world but is also a centre for whitewater rafting and treks in the Himalaya.

Trains run from Delhi to Haridwar (five hours), from where it is a 45-minute bus ride to Rishikesh. For direct overnight buses, see www.redbus.in.

○ GIBRALTAR, SPAIN

On 20 March 1969 John Lennon tied the knot with Yoko Ono on the Rock of Gibraltar, a small British territory off the southern coast of Spain. They had tried to get married in Paris a few days earlier but failed, so they flew into Gibraltar and went straight to the British Consulate to be married by a registrar. Lennon said the episode, as depicted in the song 'The Ballad of John and Yoko', was very romantic with the rock symbolising the foundation of their love.

Fly to Gibraltar from the UK with easyJet or walk across the border at La Línea in Spain (120km east of Malaga).

○ THE MIRAGE, LAS VEGAS, USA

Although money can't buy you love it *can* buy you a ticket to *Love,* the Cirque du Soleil show. Featuring remixed Beatles music by original record producer Sir George Martin (the real fifth Beatle) and his son Giles, the show plays at a specially designed theatre at the Mirage, a sprawling hotel and casino resort on the Las Vegas Strip. The opening of *Love* in 2006 reunited Paul and Ringo with the widows of George and John, who unveiled a plaque in memory of their husbands. Visitors can take a behind-the-scenes tour of the theatre and party at the psychedelic Revolution Lounge.

Another Cirque du Soleil (www.cirque dusoleil.com) show, *Michael Jackson One,* runs at Las Vegas' Mandalay Bay Resort.

○ OBERTAUERN, AUSTRIA

This ski resort in the Austrian Alps was chosen as a location to film part of the Beatles' second film, *Help!*. Legend has it that the Beatles were so stoned during filming that when George shouted his line 'Run, Ringo!' both Ringo and Paul ran over the next hill. Obertauern is located in the southern Bundesland region, 90km south of Salzburg, and is still a major ski and snowboarding resort. While filming here in 1965, the Beatles were based in the Edelweiss Hotel, which now has a spa and a children's ski centre and is close to the Lürzer Alm Chalet nightclub.

Salzburg is famous for another music giant, Mozart: each January it holds the Mozart Week Festival at the Mozarteum University.

○ BUENOS AIRES, ARGENTINA

More commonly associated with tango than Ringo, the Argentinian capital, Buenos Aires, is actually home to one of the world's biggest collections of Beatles memorabilia. Opened in 2011, the Museo Beatle in Buenos Aires is the brainchild of lifelong fan Rodolfo Vazquez, who collected over 8500 rare items including records, gadgets

GUESS THE SPOT:
A BEATLES TOUR GUIDE
WITH THE ICONIC ALBUM

and puppets. Next door to the museum is a clone of the Cavern Club, the Beatle Café and the Sala John Lennon stand-up comedy theatre. The museum is part of the Paseo La Plaza complex on Corrientes Avenue, the 'Broadway of Buenos Aires' lined with theatres, bars and tango clubs.
The Museo Beatle is open daily from 10am to midnight (from 2pm on Sunday); for details and tickets go to www.thecavern.com.ar.

❂ ABBEY ROAD, LONDON, ENGLAND

Initial ideas for the cover of the Beatles' final album included a photo shoot at Mount Everest but in the end they chose

to take six photographs at the zebra crossing right outside EMI Studios in leafy north London. The iconic cover of *Abbey Road,* featuring a barefoot McCartney, has spawned a million imitations and a few conspiracy theories concerning the death of Paul. Abbey Road Studios, where Pink Floyd and Radiohead also recorded, is closed to the public but it does run a live webcam (www.abbeyroad.com/crossing) of the crossing, where fans infuriate the beeping cars on a daily basis.
The closest tube station to Abbey Road is St John's Wood. Nearby, the Beatles Coffee Shop offers Beatles walking tours.

TOP SHAKESPEARIAN SITES

WITH 2014 HERALDING THE 450TH ANNIVERSARY OF SHAKESPEARE'S BIRTH, CELEBRATE THE BARD AT SOME OF HIS OLD HAUNTS AND BEST PLAY PLACES.

01 STRATFORD-UPON-AVON, ENGLAND

It all started on Henley Street, Stratford-upon-Avon, in 1564. In a half-timbered wattle-and-daub house on a busy thoroughfare in this Warwickshire town, William Shakespeare was brought forth into the world. The 16th-century pad could hardly have foreseen its future stardom. Now, it's one of England's most famous dwellings, converted into a museum that recreates Will's world, complete with period furnishings and a Tudor herb garden. But really, the whole town is Shakespeare-upon-Avon: pay your respects at Anne Hathaway's comely cottage (former home of his wife), Mary Arden's House (home of his mum) and the RSC Theatre, home of his living literary legacy. *The Royal Shakespeare Company is based at the Royal Shakespeare and Swan theatres in Stratford; for program see www.rsc.org.uk.*

02 VERONA, ITALY

'But soft, what light through yonder window breaks?' 'Tis likely the flash of a thousand

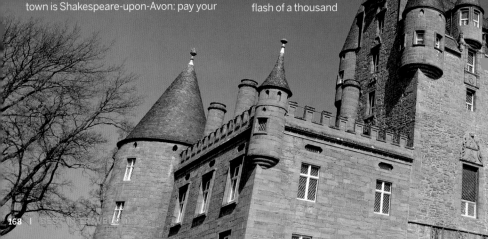

cameras! The balcony of Verona's Casa de Giulietta is not a secret spot. And though Shakespeare's teen-love tragedy was set in the city, it's rather doubtful that this humble 13th-century courtyard had anything to do with anyone who may have inspired Romeo and Juliet. But why let the truth get in the way of a good tourist attraction? Besides, with its enormous Roman amphitheatre, red-brick Castelvecchio, cobbled old streets and twisting River Adige, the city exudes plenty of real romance.

Entrance to the courtyard of Juliet's House is free; there is a fee to enter the house and stand on the balcony.

---

03 HELSINGØR, DENMARK

The first Kronberg Castle dates back to the 1420s, when it was erected on the eastern tip of Zealand to guard the narrow Øresund Strait. Then, thanks to Frederik II's fancy renovations in the late 16th century, it became one of Europe's key Renaissance fortifications. This reputation obviously travelled fast, for when penning Hamlet around 1600, Shakespeare placed his troubled prince right here. Now forever know as Elsinore, the castle has embraced its literary associations. Frequent productions of Hamlet are performed within Kronberg's walls, which over the years have seen Laurence Olivier, Derek Jacobi and Jude Law take on the role of the great Dane.

Trains runs from Copenhagen Central to Elsinore (45 minutes). Kronberg is a 15-minute walk from the station.

✪ SCOTLAND

Macbeth has a bad rep – Shakespeare did not write the 11th-century Scot well, making him out to be a power-hungry murderer with an unhinged missus. But was he really so bad? The Macbeth Trail driving route, launched in 2013, might suggest not, linking locations from Shakespeare's play to the actual man. Glamis Castle (Wills called Macbeth the 'Thane of Glamis'), Lumphanan (the Aberdeenshire village where Macbeth was killed in battle in 1057) and Cairn O'Mount (where Macbeth took his supporters en route to Lumphanan) are all on the trail – with some suitably dramatic Scottish scenery in between.

The castle and gardens at Glamis, 20km north of Dundee, are open for tours March to November (www.glamis-castle.co.uk).

ROYAL GLAMIS CASTLE IS NORTH OF DUNDEE

✪ MARUYAMA, JAPAN

Did you read the one about the Bard and the bullet train? No one did – until 1997, when some Surrey-based architects built a slice of Elizabethan England not far from Tokyo. The flashing neon of Japan's capital is still visible from Maruyama's incongruous Shakespeare Country Park. An animatronic Will welcomes bardolators to this cluster of half-timbered cottages arranged around a village green, complete with stocks and maypole. Imported British oak supports the replica birthplace, Mary Arden's house and a windmill, all constructed using traditional methods – though earthquake-proofed to suit the new location, 16,000km and five centuries away.

Shakespeare Country Park is around 80km northeast of Tokyo. The on-site theatre puts on Shakespeare's plays (in Japanese).

✪ ALEXANDRIA, EGYPT

Antony & Cleopatra is all over the place: location-wise, the play flits across the Roman Empire. But it's the scenes set in Alexandria that are the most exotic – and most tragic. In today's Mediterranean-side city, mementoes of Cleo – Queen of Egypt from 51 to 30 BC – are scant. Her royal palace was destroyed by earthquakes, and lies sunken in the ancient harbour (though an underwater museum has been mooted); the Pharos lighthouse, built by one of Cleopatra's ancestors, is likewise submerged. For now, the best bet is to promenade the Corniche, and ponder the glories that wait beneath the waves.

The Alexandria National Museum, located in an Italianate mansion on Tariq Al-Horreya St, documents the history of the city.

✪ MOUNT PÁRNITHA, GREECE

Mount Párnitha National Park has nothing to do with Shakespeare. But since the main setting of *A Midsummer Night's Dream* is a rather nonspecific 'wood outside Athens', it's as good a bet as any. It's certainly the most enchanting. While the capital's suburbs have gobbled up much surrounding countryside, this swathe of caves, gorges, peaks, trails and fir forest – just 30km to the northwest – is an accessible and surprising wilderness. Inhaling its fragrant pine, walking amid its wildflowers and gazing up to 1413m Karavola (the park's highest summit), it's easy to imagine Titania and Oberon dancing amid the trees.

Bus 714 runs from central Athens to Thrakomakedones, where a cable car runs up into Mount Párnitha National Park.

✪ VANCOUVER, CANADA

Some historians believe Francis Drake stopped by the spot we call Vancouver in 1579; most think the Spanish got there first, but not until 1791. Either way, Shakespeare would have known little of this distant western land, and certainly set no works there. Yet, each year, Vancouver celebrates Will like he's their own. Every summer since 1990 the Bard on the Beach festival has provided affordable access to Shakespeare: two stages are erected in waterfront Vanier Park, and a program of plays, talks and even a tasty bard-b-q is put on, against a breathtaking backdrop of mountains, sea and sky.

The Bard on the Beach festival runs from June to September in Vanier Park, Kitsilano; tickets and information are available from www.bardonthebeach.org.

A TIMELESS SCENE AT LONDON'S GLOBE THEATRE

⚙ MESSINA, SICILY, ITALY

Shakespeare set *Much Ado About Nothing* in Messina, northeast Sicily. A creative decision, or a hint at much more ado? In 2002 Sicilian professor Martino Iuvara put forth a theory: Shakespeare actually hailed from Messina. Iuvara alleged that young Sicilian noble Michelangelo 'Crollalanza' ('Shakespeare' in Italian) emigrated to England and went on to wed Anne Hathaway – an excellent translator. Maybe. Maybe not. But when it's drizzling in Stratford-upon-Avon, Messina's sunshine, pizzas and piazzas might seem a more attractive bard-honouring option.

Ferries connect Messina to Villa San Giovanni on Italy's mainland (20 minutes).

⚙ SHAKESPEARE'S GLOBE, LONDON, ENGLAND

The Globe, one of the first purpose-built playhouses in London, was constructed on the Southbank in 1599 – and Shakespeare was a shareholder. It burned down in 1613, during a performance of *Henry VIII* (stage cannons and thatch roofs don't mix). Sketches of the theatre are, well, sketchy. Best guesses reckon it was a 20-sided roofless polygon built of oak laths and lime plaster. In 1997, these guesses took shape and a new Globe opened, 230m from the site of the original.

The Globe's theatre season runs April to October; the exhibition and site tour is open year-round (www.shakespearesglobe.com).

WHERE TO WIN YOUR OWN WINTER OLYMPICS

CAN'T MAKE IT TO THE 2014 WINTER GAMES IN SOCHI? CREATE YOUR OWN COMPETITION BY TRYING THE COOLEST EVENTS IN THE WORLD'S BEST SPOTS.

01 SKI-JUMPING, PARK CITY, UTAH, USA

It's the Winter Olympics at its most mentally chilling: Lycra-ed figures in oversize skis hurtling down jumps, launching off at 90km/h, dangling midair, then landing safely (hopefully) on the slope below. These must be the bravest (or daftest?) athletes at the party. So join them! Utah's Olympic Park, near Salt Lake City, hosted the 2002 games. The paraphernalia's still there, with expert coaches to guide squeaky-bummed beginners off 2m-high jumps – or higher, if they dare. If not, the Extreme Zipline starts at the top of the K120 ski jump, so amateurs can experience the thrill (and terror) of making the leap. Admission to Utah Olympic Park is free; guided tours cost US$11, and run daily on the hour from 11am to 4pm.

02 FIGURE-SKATING, LAKE WEISSENSEE, CARINTHIA, AUSTRIA

Lake Weissensee may have the only skating academy based on natural ice, but it's not necessarily a good place to learn. After all, it's tough to concentrate on your double salchows when you're surrounded by such scenery: a seemingly endless frosted mere, largely untouched by tourism development and hugged by the Gailtal Alps. Distracting, to be sure, but this is the ultimate place to skate. From mid-December until early March, the 6.5 sq km lake freezes over, an ice master supervises the circular rinks (up to 25km long) and everyone from hockey players to horse-drawn-sleighers enjoys a super slide. Lake Weissensee is 120km from Klagenfurt airport. The nearest train station is Greifenburg, 12km away.

03 BOBSLEIGH, LILLEHAMMER, NORWAY

Bombing down a bobsleigh track, reaching speeds of 120km/h and facing forces of 5G really looks like something you should leave to the experts. But in the small town of Lillehammer – Norway's oldest winter resort, on the shores of Lake Mjøsa – they'll let almost anyone have a try. The 1994 Winter Games were contested here, and the

1710m-long Olympic bobsleigh run is still open for action. Tackle its turns like a pro in a four-man bob (with a pilot), or opt for a rubber bob-raft, which still hits 100km/h. In summer, wheel-bobs negate the need for ice. Lillehammer is 180km north of Oslo. The bobsleigh track is at Hunderfossen, 15km outside of town.

✿ TOBOGGAN, CRESTA RUN, ST MORITZ, SWITZERLAND

Crazy men on planks of wood have been hurling themselves down Switzerland's Cresta Run since 1885. This historic toboggan course is 1.2km long, carved afresh from the Engadine Valley's ice each year and using the landscape's natural contours to twist,

turn and plunge 157 vertical metres to the hamlet of Celerina. The course record (from top to bottom) is a frightening 50.09 seconds; beginners brave enough to try must start from the Junction, one-third down. The skill is in balancing speed and technique, using special raked boots to brake and steer round the corners – without coming an icy cropper. Cresta Run (www.cresta-run.com) is open Christmas to late February. Riders must be over 18 and male – women aren't allowed.

✿ ICE HOCKEY, TORONTO, CANADA

Ice hockey is the official sport of Canada. Indeed, the Canadians invented it in its current form in 1875. So no wonder they're

RIDING THE CRESTA RUN REQUIRES NERVES OF STEEL

pretty good – and maybe a little obsessed. Experience this adulation in Toronto: visit the Hockey Hall of Fame to see *a lot* of memorabilia, get close to the famed Stanley Cup and shoot against a virtual goalie. Then try to get a ticket for a Maple Leafs match, to watch the breakneck brutality in action. If you fancy having a go yourself, hire a stick and skates at any public rink and join a game of 'shinny' – hockey's more civilised relation.

Toronto's Hockey Hall of Fame (www.hhof. com) is open 362 days a year, 9.30/10am–6pm; adult tickets cost C$17.50.

☺ CURLING, SCOTLAND

Great Britain doesn't win many Winter Olympic medals. So when the Women's Curling Team came home with the gold in 2002, the nation got excited, even briefly obsessed by this slippery sport (think bowls on ice, with sweeping). The champs all hailed from Scotland, undoubtedly the place to give it a whirl: the Royal Caledonian Curling Club has taster sessions, which teach basic stone and broom skills. For further inspiration, the Scottish Sports Hall of Fame at Edinburgh's National Museum displays the 'stone of destiny' – the rock that clinched victory for the GB team.

Royal Caledonian Curling Club's 'Try Curling Sessions' (www.royalcaledoniancurlingclub. org/try-curling), usually free, last two hours.

☺ DOWNHILL-SKIING, NAGANO, JAPAN

There are bigger slopes, maybe even better ones. But do they have snow monkeys, hot springs and locals with a fondness for playing with fire? The deep-powder pistes at Nagano hosted the 1998 Winter Olympics, so the area has pedigree – and 35 resorts close by,

dumped with lots of snow. But it's more than that. Stay at the ancient village of Nozawa Onsen to ski by day and warm up by night – either at its 13 *sotoyu* (free public baths) or its Dosojin Fire Festival, an official 'Important Intangible Folk Cultural Property', where men of 25 or 42 flame-fight everyone else.

Trains run from Tokyo to Nagano (90 minutes); Nagano to Nozawa Onsen takes 75 minutes by bus. Dosojin is held on 15 January.

☺ SNOWBOARDING, WANAKA, NEW ZEALAND

Want the Winter Olympics to last all year long? New Zealand's slopes offer excellent boarding action from June until October, the perfect complement to a snow season spent in the north. Four mixed and marvellous ski areas ripple out from the lakeside town of Wanaka: beginners' favourite Cardrona; cross-country-focused Snow Farm; Treble Cone, for keen off-pisters; and Snow Park, for halfpiping, freestyling fiends. Better still, take your board aboard a chopper to access the biggest heli-ski area outside North America – the powder is untouched, the gradients intense and the views spectacular.

Short flights link Wanaka to Christchurch; by road the journey takes five hours. Queenstown to Wanaka is an hour's drive.

☺ CROSS-COUNTRY SKIING, VERMONT, USA

In Vermont, the hills are alive with the sound of swooshing. Just outside the charming old village of Stowe sits the Trapp Family Lodge, home of the legendary Von Trapp family singers (immortalised by Julie Andrews and co in *The Sound of Music*). The real-life clan emigrated here in 1950, bringing an Austrian

love of cross-country skiing with them. In the 1960s their Alpine-style retreat became the first Nordic resort in the country; now, 100km of trails – groomed and backcountry – criss-cross this pretty patch of New England mountain and forest. It's enough to make you burst into song...

By car the Trapp Family Lodge (www.trapp family.com) is 2.5 hours from Montréal and six hours from New York.

☼ SPEED-SKATING, RIDEAU CANAL SKATEWAY, OTTAWA, CANADA

Come winter, the Rideau Canal – which wends right through the Canadian capital – turns into the world's largest skating rink. When the mercury plummets to a consistent -10°C or less (typically January–February), a 7.8km stretch of the canal, from the Parliament Buildings to Dows Lake, becomes a-glide with Ottawans. It's a fairy-tale way to view the city. And there's no need to rush – while you could speed-skate for Olympic exercise, it's better to take it gently, stopping frequently en route: stalls selling hot chocolate are set up right on the ice-encrusted channel, so you needn't even unlace your blades for a brew.

Capital Skates (Mackenzie King Bridge) and Dows Lake Pavilion offer skate hire, Monday to Sunday, 9am/10am–10pm.

WHERE TO FEEL LIKE ONE OF THE FAMILY

WITH 2014 MARKING THE 20TH ANNIVERSARY OF THE INTERNATIONAL YEAR OF THE FAMILY, HERE'S HOW TO KIP WITH CLANS WORLDWIDE.

01 CASAS PARTICULARES, CUBA

The room is a retro revelation: all quirky antiques, faded family photos and leafy plants. A warm breeze teases through the paint-flaked shutters. The table heaves under a mountain of fresh prawns and impassioned conversation about Castro and what's going on in the soaps. Then the cigars come out... *Casas particulares* (Cuban homestays), legalised in 1997, provide vital additional income for many locals. For travellers, they provide the best way to stay on the Caribbean isle: not only cheaper than hotels, *casas* offer oodles more character, homecooked food and an instant way in to Cuban culture.

Casas particulares (www.casaparticular cuba.org) are found island-wide. Rooms are usually US$20-50 per night; meals are extra.

02 GER, MONGOLIA

Homestays in the Gobi Desert? OK, homes don't really 'stay' here: nomads shift their gers (yurts) at the whim of the weather. But some of these felt tents stay put long enough for steppe-roaming travellers to get a night of local living. There are rules: when approaching a ger, call *'Nokhoi khor!'* (Hold the dog!), the Mongolian equivalent of knocking; on entering, walk to the left (on the right is the family area); don't sit with your back or feet pointing towards the ger's altar; and when offered some *airag* (fermented mare's milk), accept – even if you'd rather not...

Ger camps open from mid-May. June and September are pleasant; July–August is peak season, though temperatures can top 40°C.

03 COCONUT PLANTATION, KERALA, INDIA

The Keralan coconut trade is not what it used to be. Prices have slumped and youngsters no longer want to spend time scampering up trees to scrape a meagre living. Luckily, the residents of God's Own Country are a resourceful lot. With the classic crop failing to raise the rupees, many plantation owners in the South Indian state have opened their colonial-cool doors to passing travellers instead. That means opportunities for intimate stays in often elegant, antique-bedecked buildings, with palms and lushness wafting outside the windows, backwaters burbling nearby and delicious (possibly coconut-infused) curries cooked each night. The main airports are at Cochin, Kozhikode and Trivandrum. The Trivandrum Rajdhani Express (Delhi to Trivandrum) takes 41 hours.

✿ TOWNSHIP HOUSE, SOWETO, JOHANNESBURG, SOUTH AFRICA

In 1904 the township of Klipspruit was established southwest of Johannesburg to house the black-African labourers that officials didn't want clogging the city. It grew exponen-tially, spawning the vast, chaotic melting-pot that is Soweto. Today it's a fascinating mix: tin shacks and shebeens (pubs) lean near glitzy malls and mansions; there's a Mandela Museum (in Nelson's former home), memorials to the 1976 student uprising, and even a distinct Soweto substyle of youth dress and lingo. Staying overnight with a local family in their township home is the best way to begin to comprehend this vibrant, tough and tenacious multicultural sprawl. Soweto is reached by MetroRail from Johannesburg Park Station. Guided tours are advised for exploring beyond Orlando West.

THE BAYANGOVI GER CAMP IN THE GOBI DESERT

✿ SOBE, CROATIA

Jump off a bus or hop off a ferry somewhere along the Croatian coast in summertime, and your first encounter is not with the lapping turquoise sea or fish-grilling tavernas, but a line of *sobe*-ladies – often wizened old grand-mas – touting rooms for rent in their homes. '*Sobe*? You want room? I give good price', is the staccato call. And they're not wrong. Although quality and style may vary (look before you pay), *sobe* are a snip, and can come with kitchenettes, cosy beds and even a surrogate mum for the duration of your stay. Arrive in town early for the greatest choice of rooms and the best bargaining position.

✿ IBAN LONGHOUSE, SARAWAK, MALAYSIA

Things can get cosy in an Iban longhouse. Members of Sarawak's largest ethnic group (once known for their headhunting procliv-ities) traditionally live in communal, wonky, wooden structures that might be home to 30-odd families – and a few curious travellers. Many longhouses are secreted away in the jungle, reached only by boat. On arrival, your first port of call should be the tribe's chief, who will hopefully grant you permission to ascend into the longhouse's *ruai* (common area). This is where it all happens: eating, rice-wine drinking, gossiping, dancing... The Iban like to party, so don't count on much sleep. Gifts should be given to Iban hosts, and easily divisible items are best – gifts will be shared among all the longhouse's families.

✿ VILLAGE HOME, OTAVALO, ECUADOR

There's no rest for the guest in the Ecuador-ean Highlands – not when there's corn to be picked or sandals to be stitched. Around the traditional town of Otavalo, known for its colourfully dressed indigenous people and (fairly touristy) handicraft market, a scatter of homesteads welcomes travellers, and encourages them get their hands dirty. Rise with the cock's crow – it's worth it to watch the sunrise over the nearby volcanoes – then spend the day helping out, feeding the guinea pigs, planting cabbage or learning Andean embroidery. Efforts will be repaid by generous meals (remember those guinea pigs?) and a more authentic Otavaleño encounter. Community-tourism operator Runa Tupari arranges homestays and cultural activities in the area; see www.runatupari.com.

✿ BEDOUIN TENT, WADI RUM, JORDAN

OK, the convivial camps that dot the Jordan-ian desert might not be 100% authentic – you'd need to know a Bedouin family well before they invited you to stay overnight. But the tourist versions still provide a starry snap-shot of this Middle Eastern lifestyle, with the welcome addition of flush loos and solar showers. Head out amid Wadi Rum's weird rocks by 4WD or camel, stopping to meet some real Bedouin for a cup of tea, and spend the night under canvas, snuggled in blankets while a campfire flickers in the sand and a canopy of constellations flickers far above. The best months to visit are March to April and October to November; from May to September temperatures can exceed 40°C.

✿ BURE, FIJI

There's not much to a traditional Fijian *bure* – a simple wood-and-thatch windowless cabin

with dark, smoky walls and a packed-earth floor. But when paradise lies just outside, no one's much concerned with interior decor. These days *bures* might have a few more amenities, but the rest is unchanged: the South Pacific is just as blue, the beaches as Bounty-ad beautiful. Better, though, is feeling part of the Fijian community. Join the ladies on a market shop, sail out with the village fishermen, learn to cook your catch in a *lovo* (earth-pit oven) or simply sit and shoot the sea breeze.

When visiting a village it's polite to give a gift of kava root to the host. For homestay options see www.fijihomestays.com.

✿ COUCH, WORLDWIDE

Beachside chalet, city apartment, bungalow, cabin, mansion, hovel – any one of these could be home for the night, anywhere on the planet. Thanks to the internet, which means you can now contact a bloke in Uzbekistan as easily as you can the man next door, the concept of couch-surfing has gone gargantuan. The idea is that when you're travelling you can get in touch with willing locals and stay in their homes for free. In exchange, you exchange: this is about cultural mixing as much as bagging a bargain.

The best-known free-sleep network is www.couchsurfing.org; similar options are www.bewelcome.org and www.hospitalityclub.org.

BEST LUXURY BOOT CAMPS

AT THESE WELLNESS RETREATS, THE STAFF WILL KICK YOUR BUTT –
AND THEN SPOIL YOU SILLY.

01 PURE KAUAI, HAWAII, USA

Use the island's stunning nature as a gym –
surf lessons, kayak excursions, rainforest
hikes and beach runs – at Pure Kauai
bespoke fitness vacations. Guests are set up
in private cottages or villas, then catered to
by personal trainers, health-minded private
chefs, personal assistants and wellness
practitioners from massage therapists to
intuitive healers and astrologists. Although
vacations can be as active or as mellow
as guests wish, the sports instructors and
personal trainers are prepared to kick it into
high gear. Quite a few celebs have stayed with
Pure Kauai to get in shape for a role.
Getting there: fly to Kauai. There is a five-
night minimum stay; www.purekauai.com.

02 THE RANCH AT LIVE OAK, MALIBU, CALIFORNIA, USA

Don't call it a spa – it's a week of tough love.
Nothing is optional: not the pre-dawn wakeup
calls for morning yoga, not the 16km to 21km
hikes every day, not the four hours of fitness
classes, and not the superstrict diet (no

meat, wheat, sugar, dairy, caffeine, alcohol or
processed foods). Participants, no more than
16 at a time, may suffer migraines or vomit on
the trail and still the instructors push them to
keep going. The results: nearly everyone loses
noticeable weight and feels better leaving than
they did when they arrived – partly from the
detox diet and partly from having survived.
Getting there: fly to Los Angeles. The program (www.theranchmalibu.com) is Sunday
to Saturday; there's also a four-day version.

03 THE ISLAND EXPERIENCE, ILHA GRANDE, BRAZIL

There's more to this island than hammocks
and *caipirinhas:* it's also home to a seven-day
program designed to detox and de-stress
through rainforest hiking, kayaking, yoga and
meditation and a vegetarian diet. In a casual
atmosphere, up to 12 guests get personal
attention and gentle encouragement, rather
than drill-sergeant discipline. The founders
created the Island Experience after a seven-
day hike around Ilha Grande that left them
wanting to share the experience with others:
not just physical challenges but also learning

to face one's limits, beat challenges, manage fears and open up to other cultures.

Getting there: fly to Rio de Janeiro. The program is Sunday to Saturday; www. theislandexperience.com.

✪ THE ASHRAM, MALLORCA, SPAIN

The seasonal program is the same as at the original Ashram in California, where celebrities have long flocked to lose weight and clear their heads. It's rigorous, to be sure: 5.30am wakeup calls for yoga; four to six hours of hiking, sometimes with nearly 1000m of elevation gain; afternoon kayaking, strength training, TRX or Pilates; more yoga; minimal, vegetarian meals; and utterly exhausted sleep. With up to 14 guests, everyone gets pushed – hard. You'll stay in a restored 17th-century olive farm surrounded by orchards and terraces with stunning views, where the guest rooms have beamed ceilings, local art and private bathrooms.

Getting there: fly to Palma. The program runs Sunday to Saturday and is held from April to June; www.theashram.com.

✪ ESCAPE TO SHAPE, INTERNATIONAL

The premier 'travelling fitness spa' combines luxury, culture and fitness in glamorous locations around the world. Each program is tailored to make the most of its location, with a focus on history, culture, people, cuisine

GET SOME WAVE THERAPY IN KAUAI'S SURF

and natural wonders – and butt-kicking. While destinations have ranged from Cape Town (where the program included African dance) to Sicily (where guests climbed Mt Etna), the setup is consistent: each day includes a total body workout that might involve yoga, Pilates, circuit training, hiking, kayaking or biking; healthy meals that reflect the region; and a bit of downtime to explore and enjoy the surroundings.

Trip length varies but is generally about a week; www.escapetoshape.com.

✿ CAL-A-VIE, VISTA, CALIFORNIA, USA

Don't let the la-di-da name and French Provençal decor fool you: the seasoned trainers here seriously kick butt. The morning mountain hike can turn into a mountain run. Guests are allowed to do as much or as little as they want, and there are a lot of beginner-friendly options among the 125 classes, but there's also CrossFit and an amped-up TRX class. The gym is as state-of-the-art as it gets and the high staff-to-guest ratio (21 trainers for up to 32 guests) ensure that anyone who asks to be challenged will be. It's not unheard-of to have one student and two instructors.

Getting there: fly to San Diego. Programs are three, four or seven days with set dates; www.cal-a-vie.com.

✿ BIKINI BOOT CAMP, TULUM, MEXICO

Founded about a decade ago, this was one of the first adventure-fitness-and-yoga programs around. The boot camps combine cool shabby-chic settings (originally the Amansala ecoresort in this yoga mecca on the Mayan Riviera and now also on Ibiza) with

activities and vacation fun. Most of the fitness classes, from power walks to cardio workouts to yoga classes, take place right on the sand and they're complemented with salsa or belly-dancing classes. Guests range from fitness newbies to hardcore gym rats and the program is tailored accordingly.

Getting there: fly to Cancún. Programs are six nights with set dates and begin on a different day each week; www.bikinibootcamp.com.

✿ THE BODYHOLIDAY, ST LUCIA

It may take willpower to make this a boot camp, as the 'holiday' part of the name is taken seriously and there are all the temptations of an all-inclusive Caribbean resort. But for guests with enough drive, there are lots of offerings that would challenge the founders – one of them a former ultramarathoner. A day may include a 7am beach boot camp class, a 4-mile run, morning aerobics, afternoon windsurfing and evening Ashtanga yoga. It all gets kicked up a notch during the WellFit retreats in March and November, when ex-Olympians and pro athletes lead the training.

Getting there: fly to St Lucia. WellFit retreats are five nights; other stays can be any length; www.thebodyholiday.com.

✿ CHIVA-SOM, HUA-HIN, THAILAND

The name means 'Haven of Life', but for guests who sign on for this destination spa's fitness retreats, life is anything but restful. There are classes nearly 12 hours a day, from Muay Thai boxing to Ashtanga yoga to a cardio session called Mountain Trek, plus private fitness assessments and an array of personal training sessions, both indoors and

REVITALISING
BODY AND SOUL
AT CHIVA-SOM SPA

out. A team of highly trained international specialists oversee the fitness and the Eastern and Western wellness services (reflexology, Thai massage, deep-tissue bodywork) that soothe sore muscles after classes are done. The healthy Thai food is delicious. Getting there: fly to Bangkok. Chiva-Som has a three-night suggested minimum; www.chivasom.com.

✿ LA RÉSERVE RAMAUTELLE, FRANCE

Just a few miles from Saint-Tropez, this resort is primarily a place for summer relaxation. But it offers a surprisingly rigorous boot camp fitness retreat, centered on the very

civilised European sport of Nordic walking (with poles, which makes it a lot harder). Each guest (no more than eight) starts with a medical assessment before embarking on a program of daily 15km to 20km treks through the mountains and along the coast, tailored to guests' fitness levels. This being France, a balanced Mediterranean diet and slimming treatments like balneotherapy (bathing in mineral-rich waters) speed up the results. Getting there: fly to La Mole. The boot camp program is five nights and available anytime from April to November; see www.lareserveramatuelle.com.

SIGHTS TO MAKE YOU FEEL SMALL

THINK YOU'RE SPECIAL? THINK AGAIN. THESE SIGHTS – TOWERING MOUNTAINS, VAST DESERTS, ENDLESS SKIES – WILL PUT YOU BACK IN YOUR PLACE.

01 MASS GAMES, PYONGYANG, NORTH KOREA

Scary and spectacular in equal measure, North Korea's Mass Games personify the country's totalitarian politics – and serve as a strikingly well-ordered reminder that we are all just one of seven-odd billion souls strutting and fretting on this globe's stage. Granted, not every earthling is gathered in Pyongyang for this event, but it sometimes seems like it: at the Games, ranks of meticulously organised dancers and gymnasts (around 100,000 in all) create a visual display not of personal skill but of perfect synchronicity. This is masses of humanity working together, greater than the sum of its parts.

The Games are held from mid-August to mid-October. September to October is less humid and more pleasant than summer in Korea.

02 RUB' AL-KHALI (EMPTY QUARTER), OMAN

If the Inuit really have a blizzard of words for snow, the Bedu of Arabia must have likewise for sand, so utterly is their world consumed and ruled by it. Smothering a fifth of the Arabian Peninsula, the Rub' al-Khali ('quarter of emptiness') is the largest sand sea in the world. Its ripples – tinged red-orange by abundant feldspar – carpet more than 580,000 sq km of Oman, Yemen, the United Arab Emirates and Saudi Arabia. Stand atop a dune, with nowt but the most perfect of deserts visible in every direction, and you'll feel as microscopic as one of those many grains of sand...

One of the easiest ways to access the Empty Quarter is by guided expedition from Salalah, southern Oman.

03 MALDIVES

The Maldives make you feel piffling at the best of times: stand on one of its ravishing atolls, and you're a speck on a speck in the Indian Ocean. But to be well and truly put in your place, jump into that paradisical blue for a close encounter with a gentle giant. The world's largest fish, whale sharks can reach up to 12m in length. Yet their plankton-eating preferences make

SIZE UP A WHALE SHARK:
THEY CAN GROW AS
LONG AS A BUS

them safe to snorkel with – although the lack of danger doesn't decrease the sense of awe. Dangle mere metres from one of these behemoths to feel very small indeed. Whale sharks travel depending on season: May to December they're seen around the western islands; December to April, they're found around the east.

✺ ATACAMA DESERT, CHILE

Sure, you can be dwarfed by mountains and deserts, but that's nothing to being dwarfed by the universe itself. In the unbeatably arid Atacama Desert, on Chile's Pacific Coast, the air is so dry that clouds rarely cause celestial obstruction, and the people are so few that scant light pollutes the night – which means there are few better places for guaranteed stargazing of truly astronomical proportions. There are powerful telescopes here if you want to zoom in, but for an overview of awesome, simply lay back and blink up at the fathomless yonder; a criss-cross of constellations, planets and who-knows-what-else will blink right back. The European Southern Observatory operates three observing sites in the Atacama Desert: La Silla, Paranal and Chajnantor.

✪ YORK MINSTER, ENGLAND

In the walled city of York, 320km north of London, construction of Europe's greatest Gothic cathedral began in 1220 and went on for a staggering 250 years. It was worth the wait. Built to a classic cruciform design, the Minster towers above York's famously narrow alleys and stout city walls. With intricate decor, spooky subterranean crypts and enormous chiming 10-tonne bells, this is cathedral design on steroids; it shows man at his most architecturally audacious, trying to reach up to God. Both its physical presence (not least the 23m-tall Great East Window) and its spiritual purpose are truly humbling.
York is crowded during the high-season summer months; an autumn visit (September to October) still provides warm days but with a fraction of the crowds.

✪ CAVE OF SWALLOWS, MEXICO

Mexico's Yucatán is like a Swiss cheese – a wholly holey land, riddled with concealed caverns. The Cave of Swallows (Sótano de las Golondrinas) is the second-biggest of these sinkholes, and one of the most dramatic. Plunging nearly 400m down amid the jungle, it could engulf the Empire State Building – not to mention the brave (or foolhardy) souls who dare to BASE jump or rappel down into its bowels. As if the scale wasn't enough to make you feel puny, you're also outnumbered: this Hadean realm is favoured by thousands of white-collared swifts, which leave the cave at dawn and return at dusk in overwhelming avian swarms.
The Cave of Swallows is 13km from the village of Aquismón, just off Hwy 85 in the Huasteca region.

✪ GREAT AUSTRALIAN BIGHT, AUSTRALIA

Cliff upon cliff upon cliff upon cliff… Looking east from the frontier-feel town of Eucla along Australia's barren south coast, there seems to be no end to this monster sea wall: with 60m- to 120m-high jags of pale sedimentary rock, the Great Australian Bight stretches largely uninterrupted for more than 1000km of emptiness. Well, it's empty-ish. Though backed by the equally lonely Nullarbor Plain, a surprising diversity of life has evolved to handle the hostile conditions: sea lions on the beaches, leafy sea dragons amid the kelp, platoons of southern right whales huffing offshore. Humans, however, are rarely seen – the Bight is more than man can chew…
Watch southern right whales from the coast at the Head of Bight lookout, 78km west of Yalata (South Australia), July to September.

✪ TANE MAHUTA (LORD OF THE FOREST), WAIPOUA FOREST, NEW ZEALAND

It's not often you get to meet a god. But in the titanic kauri forests of far north New Zealand it's easy to believe you're among deities: here, these truly colossal trees soar more than 50m high, dwarfing those who delve between them. Two venerable trees dominate the Waipoua Forest: Te Matua Ngahere (Father of the Forest) presides over a clearing, but a little further north Tane Mahuta holds court. Named after the Maori forest god, the largest living kauri has stretched to 51m in height in its 1200-plus years. Hush, and be awed. As if you have a choice.
These beautiful trees are threatened by the kauri dieback disease; clean your shoes before and after visiting each forest.

✿ STROMBOLI, ITALY

Lest you forget our planet has a molten core, this volatile Italian isle will set you straight. Known as the 'Lighthouse of the Mediterranean' for its eruptive activity, Stromboli is part of the Aeolian Islands, an archipelago of seven volcanic peaks off the north coast of Sicily. The most awesome of the islands, Stromboli belches regular explosions of dust and steam, spitting rocks and, at times, lava down the barren Sciara del Fuoco trail into the Mediterranean Sea. Find a fisherman to take you out on the water at dusk to watch the natural pyrotechnics at their bellowing best. Stromboli has no airport. Reach the Aeolians by ferry from Naples, or Milazzo on Sicily.

✿ CONCORDIA, PAKISTAN

This might well be the pudding bowl of the gods, a scooped-out icy enclave with gargantuan sides where every direction yields a terrifying, 8000m-plus peak. In the recesses of Concordia you will feel really, really small. It's a long trek into this sparkling basin, about a week from the trailhead near Skardu. But those who make it don't regret it; to have their existence questioned by the icy face of Gasherbrum, the avalanches of Broad Peak, the creaking Baltoro Glacier shifting eerily underfoot and the might of K2 lording over it all. Skardu is a 20- to 24-hour drive from Islamabad via the Karakoram Highway. Islamabad–Skardu flights take one hour.

BEST PLACES TO GET DRESSED FOR SUCCESS

ANYONE CAN BUY READY-TO-WEAR. BUT THE SAVVIEST TRAVELLERS GET THINGS MADE TO ORDER, LOCAL-STYLE.

01 SARIS, MUMBAI, INDIA

In emerald greens, peacock blues, royal purples, sunrise oranges and pomegranate reds, saris delightfully symbolise India's colourful culture and landscape. On the subcontinent, sari seekers generally buy the garments at specialty fabric shops and have the choli (the cropped shirt traditionally worn with some styles of sari) made at an on-site or nearby tailor. For selection, you can't beat Kala Niketan, an overstuffed Mumbai emporium hawking saris in silks and cottons, saris covered in delicate embroidery or adorned with simple gold borders, saris decorated with birds, with flowers, with sequins. Can't decide? Buy two (or three)!

Kala Niketan (www.kalaniketangroup.com) is on Queens Rd in the Marine Lines area of Mumbai.

02 SUITS, SHIRTS AND DRESSES, KOWLOON, HONG KONG, CHINA

When you hop off the Star Ferry and plunge into the teeming streets of Hong Kong's Kowloon peninsula, touts will immediately rush to your side asking 'Tailor? Tailor? Need a tailor?' Well, do you? This frenetic international city has long been known for its quick, nimble-fingered tailors, who can turn out a full suit or dress in less than 24 hours. Do as the locals do, and bring your nicest shirt or pair of trousers to have them 'copied' into multiple versions in multiple different materials.

In-the-know locals swear by Raja Fashions (www.raja-fashions.com) on Cameron Rd.

03 SUITS, SAVILE ROW, LONDON, ENGLAND

The poshest of the poshies have their bespoke suits made here on the 'golden mile of tailoring', famed for dressing everyone from Winston Churchill to James Bond since the early 1800s. In London's exclusive Mayfair district, Savile Row has more than a dozen tailors specialising in upper-upper-tier menswear. Go for a classic English look with a boldly striped three-piece or a classic tweed.

New kid on the block Cad and the Dandy (www.cadandthedandy.co.uk) outsources some of its processes to China to offer bespoke clothing at a lower price point, with suits starting at £950.

✪ JEANS, USA

Invented by dry goods store owner Levi Strauss during San Francisco's gold-rush years, blue jeans have become the most iconic – and ubiquitous – of American fashions. Since most of us spend more time in our jeans than any other item of clothing, it makes sense to get a pair that fit like a second skin. That's where bespoke jeans come in. A growing trend across the US, outfitters large and small are offering made-to-order denim in the cut and colour of your choice.

Levi's does made-to-order at its store in NYC's Meatpacking District (www.us.levi. com). In Nashville, Imogene & Willie (www. imogeneandwillie.com) does retro shades of indigo in a former gas station.

✪ QIPAO, SHANGHAI, CHINA

What's more elegant than the *qipao*, the slim, high-necked dress worn to such stylish effect in Hong Kong director Wong Kar-wai's 2000 film *In the Mood for Love?* Traditionally, the *qipao* (also known as *cheongsam*) was a loose garment, but socialites and high-class courtesans in racy 1920s Shanghai helped evolve it into the slinky dress of today. Shanghai is still the best place to have a *qipao* made, and the iconic tailor shop Han Yi is the top choice for in-the-know fashionistas. Choose from hundreds of fabrics, plain or embroidered, and be fitted by the shop's expert tailors. One week later, you'll look like you're ready to drink a martini at the bar of the storied Cathay Hotel circa 1932.

Han Yi is at 221 Changle Rd in the Luwan District.

FABULOUS SARI FABRI
AT A TEXTILE FACTORY
RAJASTH

☺ BRAS, PARIS, FRANCE

Everyone wonders how French women achieve their classic, effortlessly elegant looks. Well, turns out they start with a proper foundation: custom-fitted, custom-made bras, *mais oui!* At Cadolle, the legendary lingerie atelier, the Cadolle family has been making *soutien-gorges* for everyone from European royalty to the infamous spy Mata Hari. Make an appointment to get your décolleté outfitted in the finest silks and laces, all measured and cut to order over a series of fittings. They don't come cheap, but take another tip from the French: you get what you pay for and quality clothes are worth the price.

Cadolle (www.cadolle.com) is on Rue Saint-Honoré in the 1st arrondissement.

☺ GUAYABERAS, MIAMI, FLORIDA, USA

Legend has it this iconic Caribbean and Latin American shirt was invented by the wife of an old man who loved picking guavas (*guayabas*) and needed some pockets to hold them. The *guayabera,* distinguished by its four front pockets and two rows of pleating, is almost a uniform for Cuban men of a certain age in Miami, and its retro look has become newly cool among a younger crowd as well. Tailor Ramon Puig ('king of the *guayaberas*') made shirts for the likes of Ernest Hemingway and Bill Clinton for 60-plus years before passing away in 2011. Today his store sells ready-to-wear and custom *guayaberas* with delicate embroidery. Stop by and get fitted on your way to the bars of South Beach.

Ramon Puig (www.ramonpuig.com) is at 5840 SW 8th St in West Miami.

☺ SANDALS, ATHENS, GREECE

Greeks have been rocking sandals since the days of the Peloponnesian War. When in Athens, do as the Athenians do and pick up a custom-made pair, just the thing for island-hopping in the Aegean. In Greece's capital, the Melissinos family has been making sandals of gorgeous, pliable Cretan leather for nearly a century. Stop by their shop to have the sandals – shaved, moulded and oiled with local olive oil – fitted to your feet on the spot. They were good enough for Jackie O, Princess Diana, John Lennon, Sophia Loren and Jeremy Irons, and we're certain they'll be good enough for you.

Find Melissinos (www.melissinos-art.com) near Monastiraki Sq.

☺ LEATHER GLOVES, MILAN, ITALY

From the grandpa sipping grappa in the corner bar to the chic young woman riding a Vespa in 6-inch heels, Italians just seem to have a certain flair. In Milan, the country's fashion capital, located in the chilly north, handsome custom-made gloves are a major part of the equation. Sermoneta, on Milan's Via della Spiga, has been making fine gloves for more than 50 years. Just one pair, which come in materials from kidskin to deerskin to peccary (a kind of wild South American pig), takes the work of 10 separate artisans. Go ahead, live *la dolce vita* and treat yourself to a pair.

Sermoneta (www.sermonetagloves.com) is on Via della Spiga in the Quadrilatero d'Oro, Milan's upscale fashion district.

✿ COWBOY BOOTS, AUSTIN, TEXAS, USA

In Texas, cowboy boots are considered appropriate attire for everything from roping broncos to black tie galas at the governor's mansion. So it's no wonder that Austin, the capital of the Lone Star State and where traditional Texas meets the avowedly alternative, is also the world's capital of handmade cowboy boots. Get 'em in ostrich or alligator, vintage-style or cheekily modern, with fancy stitching or classic plain. Heritage Boots is a hipster favourite, selling self-described 'fancy boots', Capitol Saddlery attracts a more old-school crowd and Texas Custom Boots satisfies rockabilly types with exotic leathers like eel skin and glitzy inlays of feathers and diamonds. Giddy-up now and ride 'em, cowboy!

The shopping website Racked (www. racked.com) offers a handy map of Austin's top boot shops, including those mentioned here. Search the site for 'Where to Shop Cowboy Boots in Austin'.

HIDDEN FOODIE HIGHLIGHTS

SAVOUR THESE DELICIOUSLY OFF-BEAT TRADITIONAL SPECIALTIES AND GET A TRUE TASTE OF THE LOCAL CULTURE TO BOOT.

01 HOT DOG, CHICAGO, USA

Throw out any misgivings you might have about the plebeian hot dog – Chicago's version of this all-American classic is an all-beef affair, spiced with mustard, pickle relish and celery salt, topped with fresh diced tomatoes and onions, a pickle spear and hot sport peppers. This truly indigenous food is said to be the invention of the Windy City's enterprising residents and their multicultural heritage of European, Jewish and Mediterranean roots. No ordinary hot dog, a tasty frankfurter and salad encased in a soft poppy-seed bun makes this one elegant snack.

Tuck into an authentic Chicago-style hot dog at one of the city's many Vienna Beef hot-dog stands; www.viennabeef.com.

02 VINCISGRASSI, LE MARCHE, ITALY

The Marchigianis' take on lasagne is not for the faint of heart, turbo-charged with no less than 12 layers of slippery soft pasta sheets enriched with *vino cotto,* interspersed with a rich veal ragout spiked with chicken livers, lamb sweetbreads, truffles and wild mushrooms, all blanketed with a velvety béchamel sauce and grated parmesan cheese. The name is said to come from Austrian General Windisch Graetz, whose army helped liberate the regional capital, Ancona, from the French in the 18th century. Unsurprisingly, this baked dish of epic proportions is largely reserved for special occasions and the height of truffle season. Simpler versions of the original can be enjoyed in the city of Macerata's many charming *osterie.*

03 ADOBO, THE PHILIPPINES

It's hard to believe a dish with only four ingredients could taste so good *and* unify a nation. The Philippines' 7000-plus islands are agreed in their love for the national dish of *adobo* – a satisfyingly savoury meat stew seasoned only with garlic, soy sauce and vinegar. Served with plain boiled rice, the humble *adobo* is a lunch or dinner staple and a standard offering at office canteens and *carinderia* (street stalls) across the country. Each household, city and province

will have their own chicken or pork variations with additional ingredients such as chicken livers, peppercorns or bay leaves but a classic chicken *adobo* is the country's firm favourite.

Whip up your own *adobo* with this recipe from the Food Network (www.foodnetwork. com, search for Filipino chicken *adobo*).

☼ LOBSTER, CUBA

Cuba might be economically poor but its embarrassment of cultural riches, intriguing political history and impressive health and education systems continue to attract curious tourists to the enigmatic island.

Better-known for its music, cigars and rum, food is largely a secondary consideration for the majority of Cubans so food lovers are often in for a surprise when they discover an abundance of lobster, still largely a delicacy in the West. Typically grilled in the half shell and smothered in lemon and butter, the local lobster is fleshy yet sweet and best of all, comes supersized and supercheap in the country's state-run restaurants.

Check out the iconic Los Nardos Restaurant in Havana for generously sized lobsters at mind-bogglingly decent prices.

⊘ FIDEUÀ, CATALONIA, SPAIN

Fideuà is the Catalonian version of one of Spain's best-known culinary exports, paella. In place of rice, short, thin, vermicelli-like noodles called *fideus* are steeped in a saffron- and tomato-infused fish broth and topped with fresh seafood, including prawns, squid and shellfish, and a dollop of rich aioli. *Fideuà* is a feast for the senses with its eye-popping golden hue and heady smells of garlic and the sea. Catalans love nothing more than sharing the dish among family and friends and washing it down with generous jugs of cava or white wine in a convivial atmosphere.

The cities of Cambrils and Palamos boast some of the finest *fideuà*, including at Bell Port on 1 Passeig del Mar in Palamos.

⊘ KHACHAPURI, SOCHI, RUSSIA

Those hotfooting it to Sochi for the 2014 Winter Olympics are in for a cheesy treat with a local specialty, *khachapuri*. A cross between pide and pizza, this traditional Georgian yeast bread is a labour of love, hand-kneaded twice and baked in a very hot clay oven. Filled and topped with a rather salty local cheese called *sulguni,* an authentic *khachapuri* is blistered, puffy and flaky, with a chewy texture and the lip-smacking savoury goodness of a melted cheese sandwich. *Khachapuri* are typically enjoyed on their own or with a tarragon and walnut salad, or as a hearty side dish.

Cafe Natasha in Sochi city serves a diet-busting supersize version oozing with butter and melted cheese and an egg on top.

⊘ ODEN, JAPAN

Everyone knows about ramen, udon and soba but it is *oden* that the Japanese turn to when in need of hot and soothing comfort food. This winter staple comprises a soup in which ingredients are slowly simmered, including tofu, fish cakes, eggs, vegetables and meat. The soy base lends the dish its characteristic but unflattering shade of brown, but don't let that put you off – good *oden* has a delicate yet complex-flavoured broth and a spread of foods with a variety of tastes and textures, which can be found in Japan's many atmospheric *oden* restaurants. Top tip: the convenience store version is best avoided.

Sample exotic delicacies in one of Tokyo's oldest *oden* restaurants, Otafuku.

⊘ INCIR DOLMASI, TURKEY

Cheekily referred to by locals as 'Turkish Viagra', the sticky sweet walnut-stuffed figs are a favourite dessert and snack found in street food stalls all over the country. Soft dried figs are studded with cloves, stuffed with a whole walnut, then gently poached in a cinnamon-flavoured sugar syrup. Like the savoury *dolma* (vegetables filled with rice or meat), *incir dolması* are a hallmark of the stuffed foods of Turkey's much-lauded Otto-man cuisine. Whether the figs live up to their nickname is a moot point, but one thing is for sure: they go down a treat with Turkish coffee.

Learn how to make your own at home at the A La Turka cookery school in İstanbul (www.cookingalaturka.com).

⊘ NEM, NEW CALEDONIA

Dubbed Tropical France, the tiny island of New Caledonia enjoys a reputation as a gourmet destination with its French, Melanesian and Pacific influences creating an original and fascinating fusion cuisine. The capital city, Noumea, is a hotbed of international restaurants but locals in need of a quick snack devour *nem*, New Caledonia's take on the humble spring roll. Wonton wrappers or sheets of rice paper are filled with broken rice or noodles, mince and vegetables, shaped into finger-sized rolls and deep-fried, resulting in incredibly more-ish, satisfying savoury bites.

Nem are best eaten hot, straight from the deep fryer, and can be bought from street vendors throughout the city.

✪ CHICKEN PARMIGIANA, MELBOURNE, AUSTRALIA

Despite its Italian origins, Melburnians have adopted this chicken, cheese and ham classic with such gusto that it has become the standard by which locals judge a good pub. The perfect 'chicken parma' is a crisply crumbed, tender chicken fillet, offset by melted cheese and salty ham, and served with an unctuous homemade tomato sauce. True parma devotees engage in pub and parma crawls, and debating the merits (or otherwise) of what makes good parma over a 'pot' of beer is the best way to get in on the local action.

Try classic and modern parmas at Mrs Parma's on 25 Little Bourke St, Melbourne.

A BOWL OF ODEN HAS MANY DELICIOUS DELIGHTS

BEST CLASSIC CAR RIDES

CLASSIC CARS DON'T JUST LOOK COOL, THEY CAN PUT THE SOUL INTO A JOURNEY. PUT YOUR FAVOURITE MUSIC ON AND FASTEN YOUR SEATBELTS – IT'S ROADRUNNER TIME.

01 VOLKSWAGEN CAMPER, UK

The Volkswagen Type Two campervan was the hippy traveller's favourite vehicle: even cartoon stoners the Fabulous Furry Freak Brothers had one. Now the 'Veedub' campervan has found a new role in Britain's glamping ('glamorous camping') sector, and you can't deny that cheery 'drop life and drive' charm. All providers share certain rules: Veedubs must have a name and they must be in bright colours. Cornwall Campers' Ella, for instance, is pea-green and has Calor gas, a fridge and a sink. Pack a surfboard, wave to fellow 'dubbers' and you'll have a ball. You can find Cornwall Campers at www.cornwallcampers.co.uk.

02 TRABANT, GERMANY

With a two-stroke engine, fibreglass body and an instantly likeable car-face, the 'Trabi' was the great East German workhorse. Citizens would wait for years to buy one, then keep it going with string if need be – and with just three million produced, owning one made you an Eastern Bloc aristocrat. There are Trabi hire places in Eastern Europe, all trading on various shades of 'Ostalgie' – the jokey nostalgia for Communist-era style – but Berlin's Trabi Safari leads the way, letting you drive a Trabi around this uncongested capital city, with an affectionate commentary that hits the mood. It's a great way to see Berlin – but you won't burn off any Audis at the lights. Try Trabi Safari in Berlin or Dresden, www.trabi-safari.de.

03 CITROËN 2CV, FRANCE

The Citroën 2CV – that's two 'chevaux', as in horsepower – ceased production in 1990 after 42 years, its corrugated-steel body and low speed ('0 to 60 in one day', went the joke) loveable but obsolete. Now this car makes the French weep bittersweet tears, for it mobilised the peasantry in the postwar years. Put simply, they love it. Drive a 2CV in France and you'll get smiles from other French drivers (a hard-won treat); you'll find them for hire across France. Memo: if you're thinking about a long 2CV road trip, consider that the suspension is not kind to backsides – and that you'll have to prise nostalgic farmers off it in villages.

Manstouch (www.manstouch.com) offers tours of Paris in a fleet of reconditioned 2CVs.

✿ FIAT 500, ITALY

There are few cars that make you go 'aww' – as you would at a cute animal. The classic Fiat 500 is one of them. The earliest model was nicknamed the 'Topolino' or 'grey mouse' and was the original small car;

between 1957 and 1975 over three million Fiat 500 were produced. In those *dolce vita* years it was not uncommon to see whole families in them; now it's more likely to be a cool designer type. Or you, as specialty Italian car-hire companies, like Rome500 in Rome, offer the chance to be elegantly chauffeured by Fiat 500 in Rome. You can also self-drive to Rome's side trips, like Ostia Antica, Villa Adriana or Lake Bracciano. Tall drivers beware.

Rome500 has a range of packages with its Fiat 500 fleet at www.rome500exp.com.

A VINTAGE VOLKSWAGEN VAN IS PART OF THE GLAMPING LIFESTYLE IN WATERGATE BAY, CORNWALL

☼ MUSTANG ON ROUTE 66, USA

'Take the highway that's the best...' Classic rhythm and blues song 'Route 66' is the best road song ever, and driving a classic American car is an event in itself. Also, inner cities aside, the US was made for driving. So any serious motorist will love the Mother Road, which famously 'winds from Chicago to LA'. Hire a car from Blacktop Candy's and you can choose from a range including a 1964 Corvette Stingray and a 1965 Mustang convertible. En route you'll find vintage hotels and attractions serving drivers, including the El Rey Inn in Santa Fe and Blue Swallow Motel in Tucumcari. It's a slice of true Americana.

Classic cars are hired by Blacktop Candy's in North Carolina; www.blacktopcandys.com.

☼ ASTON MARTIN IN SCOTLAND

Despite reaching 50 last year, the appeal of top cinematic spook James Bond keeps growing. The half-Scottish Bond drove several cars, but it is the Aston Martin DB5 CHK that has become indelibly linked with 007, and Scotland is the perfect place to drive an Aston. You'll zip past Faslane Naval Base, featured in *The Spy who Loved Me,* the loch by Crinan, which stood in for the Bosphorus in *From Russia with Love,* and the reeling landscape of Glencoe, setting for the finale of *Skyfall.* You'll have speed, sexiness and (temporary) bragging rights. What you won't have is pop-out gun barrels or a bullet shield behind the rear windscreen. So pretend.

See Scotland Differently hires its Aston Martin for weekends. See www. seescotlanddifferently.co.uk.

☼ MINI MOKE, BARBADOS

The Mini Moke is proof that the Mini and the Land Rover did have an affair in the 1960s. And this rugged little looker was the result, produced in small numbers in the UK between 1964 and '68 before being made in Australia and Portugal. Sure, it didn't set the world alight in rainy climes, but it is now the coolest and most covetable beach-hopping buggy in the world, which is why the Moke is mega in Barbados. Grab one of these open-sided micro-jeeps and you'll have yourself an island adventure.

There's a list of Moke hire outfits at www. funbarbados.com (be aware: they may be updated models).

☼ THE AMBASSADOR, INDIA

Some cars are so linked with their countries that it becomes a duty to ride. So it is with the Hindustan Ambassador: the first car to be made in India (in 1948) and the titan of that country's incredible road system. It has real retro charm and is still made in West Bengal. The Amby has traversed mountains, deserts, plains and parks, taken on the monsoon, faced down roads full of people, carts, cows, elephants and yawning potholes. If you want to drive one, it's possible – but be very careful and learn to honk your horn. Better to be driven; the back seat is extremely comfy and usually has natty antimacassars.

You can take an Amby taxi or a special tour, such as those organised by Road Trip India (www.roadtripindia.co.uk).

☼ MERCEDES 250, GERMANY

There's something about the classic 1960s Mercedes 250 that really gets people going.

**A LAND ROVER ON SAFARI,
IN DAMARALAND**

Perhaps it's that it brought that Mercedes coolness to a wider market, or that it's one of the comfiest rides in the world. From that Greek temple radiator to the discreet tailfins of earlier models (between 1959 and 1968 is best), it's a looker. Hire one in southern Germany, and you'll soar past the mountains and the Black Forest. As hire provider Oldie Garage of Bavaria puts it, a key advantage is that you'll 'enjoy the admiring looks of your fellow men and ladies'. Can't be bad.

Oldie Garage (www.oldie-garage.com) is one of several hirers in business.

☼ LAND ROVERS IN AFRICA

Once in everyone's life, they should drive a 4WD Land Rover. In Namibia, you can pick up one of these Brit beauties in the capital, Windhoek, and self-drive into some of the most wonderful and weird terrain in the world: vast orange ergs, looming shipwrecks, avoiding meerkats in Damaraland. The operator Safari Drive makes sure that you have satnav and a satellite phone, and most importantly, full picnic gear. (You'll stay in campsites and lodges, so don't fret.)

Get the trip details at www.safaridrive.com.

THE CAT'S MEOW

EVERY DAY, MILLIONS OF FELINE FANATICS CLICK ON CAT VIDEOS AND CAT MEMES. TIME TO GET OFFLINE AND ON THE ROAD WITH THIS CAT-CENTRIC ITINERARY.

 CAT CAFES, JAPAN
Japan is known for many things, but lots of living space isn't one of them. Cramped quarters haven't stopped the Japanese from craving cat company, but short of collecting Hello Kitty figurines, what can a feline freak do? Enter the cat cafes, which are exactly as the name suggests. For a cover charge, patrons get a caffeine-n-cat fix, snuggling, romping or just ogling as many as two dozen fluffballs for anywhere up to six hours on end. Though the concept originated in Taiwan, cat cafes are whoppingly popular in Japan, with 150 of them nationwide.
Of more than 40 cat cafes in Tokyo alone, the most popular are Calico (www.catcafe.jp) and Cat Café Nekorobi (www.nekorobi.jp).

 HEMINGWAY'S CATS, KEY WEST, USA
Hardboiled hombre and all-round man's man Ernest Hemingway was so smitten by kittens that he called them 'love sponges'. And none soaked up more of the author's adoration than a six-toed Maine Coon named Snowball. Dozens of Snowball's descendants live on at Hemingway's gorgeous estate, now a historic museum. With distinguished lineage and names such as Elizabeth Taylor and Charlie Chaplin, these pampered pusses rule the roost, revelling in rubberneckers' affection and their celebrity status. Even their drinking fountain is famous: a urinal Papa lugged home in a stupor from his favourite bar.
Admission to the Ernest Hemingway Home and Museum (www.hemingwayhome.com) in Old Town Key West includes a guided tour and all the cats you can pat.

 THE CAT BOAT, AMSTERDAM, NETHERLANDS
The owl and the pussycat may have gone to sea, but it's a rare cat that gets on a boat for love, money *or* honey. But they do things a little differently in Amsterdam, home to the Poezenboot (Cat Boat), a floating shelter for scores of stray and abandoned cats. Docked along the Singel canal, the Poezenboot welcomes meowser-mad visitors, volunteers and those looking to adopt their own sailor cat. While in town, pop into the Katten

Kabinet, a canal-side museum that houses a rich collection of cat-themed artwork by the lofty likes of Picasso and Rembrandt.
The Cat Boat (www.poezenboot.nl) is closed on Sunday and Wednesday. Nearby Katten Kabinet (www.kattenkabinet.nl) is open daily.

✪ CAT CITY, KUCHING, BORNEO

Kuching means 'Cat City' in Malay; nobody will look sideways at those who hug street strays or shriek 'pusspusspuss!' at random moggies. Malaysia's cleanest city, Kuching was actually named after a local fruit dubbed 'cat's eye', a fact conveniently overlooked in favour of a feline flavour. Gigantic cat statues dot the landscape, hawkers flog cat carvings in local bazaars, and the Cat Museum – enter through the gaping cat mouth – is home to an astonishing 2000 artefacts (including an Egyptian mummified cat) and a research centre for cat-based religions and cat history. Frequent flights go to Kuching daily from KL and Singapore. Search for 'Cat Museum' at www.virtualmalaysia.com.

✪ PUSS PATROL, HERMITAGE, RUSSIA

Some of the most beautiful objets d'art at Russia's most opulent museum can be found in the dim corners of its dusty basement: the Hermitage cats, guardians of the palace's treasures and ratters extraordinaire. More than 50 cats make up the 'feline corps'; their predecessors first arrived in 1745 when Catherine the Great had a carriage-load of 'virile cats particularly good at mousing' delivered to the palace. Visitors can fuss over the great guards in the museum's sunny courtyards. Don't miss the annual Day of the Hermitage Cat, to be held in April 2014.
The Hermitage Museum (www.hermitagemuseum.org) is on Palace Sq by the Neva River.

COBBLESTONE CATS, KOTOR, MONTENEGRO

Montenegro is fast gaining a reputation as the crème de la crème in glamorous Mediterranean destinations. And where there's cream, there's cats... The ancient coastal town of Kotor is, for reasons unknown, a stray-cat stamping ground, with innumerable kitties posing photogenically around the old town and its Unesco-listed medieval attractions. Cats are so ubiquitous that they've become the unofficial symbol of Kotor; you may not be able to scoop one up and tote it home, but local artisans have softened the blow of separation, with lovely handmade cat creations on sale in the walled town's atmospheric laneways.

Kotor is easily reached from the capital, Podgorica, and is a day trip from the nearby cities of Herceg Novi and Dubrovnik in Croatia.

AVERAGE JOE CAT SHOW, ARLINGTON, WASHINGTON, USA

Unlike hoity-toity displays of pedigree fluff, the Average Joe Cat Show is a celebration of middling moggies. Held in Arlington, Snohomish County, the annual event pays homage to the everyday puss in categories such as Most Impressive Ear Hair, Most Obnoxious and Biggest Feet. This is a gentle, stress-free show attracting quotidian-cat fanciers from far and wide; if Washington is too far this year, hop online to gawk at photo competition entrants in classes including Best Cat in a Box and Guiltiest-Looking Cat. 'Basically, cats are freaks,' says organiser Connie Gabelein. 'And we honour that at the show.'

Arlington is 76km north of Seattle. The 11th Average Joe Cat Show (www.averagejoe catshow.org) will be held in May 2014.

MOGGIE MECCA, EGYPT

The Sphinx. Cat mummies. The cult of Bastet. Egypt is ground zero for folks that are crackers for cats. Once upon a time, all cats were owned by the Pharaoh, women and men wore makeup to mimic cats' eyes, and killing a cat was punishable by death. Today, their slightly more scruffy scions roam the hectic Cairo streets, but their regal legacy lives on in myriad tomb paintings, cat statues and millions of souvenirs from the gimcrack to the genuine. The Cairo-based Egyptian Mau Rescue Organisation even arranges international adoptions of the majestic meowsers.

Visit the Egyptian Mau Rescue Organisation (www.emaurescue.org) in person. Also check out www.ancientegyptonline.co.uk/cat for more feline facts.

BURMESE CATS, INLE LAKE, MYANMAR

Myanmar's Inle Lake is renowned for the leg-rowing fishermen who ply its picturesque waters, but another group of local fish-fanciers is attracting worldwide attention. The Burmese cat – hailed as sacred in ancient times but now almost nonexistent in its homeland – is making a comeback at the lakeside Inthar Heritage House. The cultural centre is home to a breeding program that's re-introducing the coveted cats to Myanmar: one was even given to Aung San Suu Kyi. But you don't need to be a global icon to appreciate the beauty of the Burmese: Inthar is open to

visitors, who cuddle the pedigree pusses and watch them enjoy their rice dinners. Inle Lake is served by flights and buses from Yangon, Bagan and Mandalay. Find out more at www.intharheritagehouse.com.

☺ CAT ISLAND, TASHIROJIMA, JAPAN

If you idolise cats, you'll be in good company on Japan's Tashirojima Island. Known as Cat Island, it's a far-flung haven that's heaven for felines, with a holy cat shrine, cat-shaped monuments and buildings adorned with pointy ears and whiskers. The free-roaming puss population easily outnumbers the 70-odd human residents, who believe that being kind to kitties brings good luck. The cats were originally shipped to the island to hunt mice; these days, they're more likely to be chasing down smooches and snacks from visitors. Limited camping and sleeping spots in a manga-cat-themed 'resort' are sporadically available for the truly cat-crazed. Daily ferries leave Ishinomaki City for Tashiro-jima. Email issightsee@city.ishinomaki.lg.jp to book accommodation.

INDEX

Aa

Antarctica 14-17, 152-3

Argentina 166-7

Australia 56-9, 126-9, 142, 186, 195

Austria 166, 172

Bb

Bahamas 165

Barbados 198

Belgium 38-41, 140, 160, 161, 162, 163

Belize 144-5

Bosnia & Hercegovina 162

Brazil 10-13, 148-9, 180-1

Bulgaria 137

Cc

Canada 118-21, 170, 173-4, 175

Cape Verde 158

Chile 151, 152, 185

China 84-7, 114-17, 154, 188, 189

Cook Islands 157-8

Croatia 178

Cuba 98-101, 176, 193

Czech Republic 146

Dd

Denmark 144, 169

Dominican Republic 154

Ee

Ecuador 178

Egypt 170, 202

England 60-3, 142, 164, 167, 168, 171, 186, 188

Ethiopia 139

Ff

Fiji 138, 178-9

Finland 147

France 94-7, 140, 142, 152, 161, 162, 163, 183, 190, 196-7

Gg

Germany 141, 164, 196, 198-9

Greece 136, 153, 170, 190

Grenada 158

Hh

Honduras 154-5

Ii

Iceland 146-7

India 52-5, 138, 145, 165-6, 176-7, 188, 198

Indonesia 150

Italy 136, 140, 143, 146, 168, 171, 187, 190, 192, 197

Jj

Japan 64-7, 170, 174, 194, 200, 203

Jordan 178

Ll

Latvia 106-9

Mm

Macedonia 42-5

Malawi 26-9

Malaysia 46-9, 178, 201

Maldives 184-5

Mexico 30-3, 138, 182, 186

Mongolia 176

Montenegro 202

Morocco 149

Myanmar 155, 202-3

Nn

Namibia 199

Netherlands 200-1

New Caledonia 194-5

New Zealand 80-3, 130-3, 151, 174, 186

North Korea 184

Norway 172-3

Oo

Oman 184

Pp

Pakistan 187

Palau 156

Panama 142

Papua New Guinea 158

Philippines 139, 192-3

Portugal 138

Rr

Russia 154, 194, 201

Ss

São Tomé & Príncipe 156-7

Scotland 18-21, 169, 174, 198

Seychelles 34-7, 158-9

South Africa 102-5, 177

Spain 76-9, 149, 166, 181, 194

St Lucia 149, 182

St Vincent & the Grenadines 159

Sweden 22-5

Switzerland 110-13, 173

Tt

Thailand 144, 182-3

Tonga 88-91, 156

Trinidad & Tobago 157

Turkey 141, 148, 160, 194

Uu

UK (*see also* England, Scotland) 60-3, 196

USA 68-71, 122-5, 142, 145-6, 146, 150, 151, 153-4, 164-5, 166, 172, 174-5, 180, 182, 189, 190, 191, 192, 198, 200, 202

Zz

Zambia 72-5

Zimbabwe 72-5

ACKNOWLEDGEMENTS

PUBLISHING DIRECTOR Piers Pickard
PUBLISHER Ben Handicott
PROJECT MANAGER & COMMISSIONING
EDITORS Robin Barton, Bridget Blair
ART DIRECTION Mark Adams
DESIGN Leon Mackie
LAYOUT DESIGNERS Carlos Solarte,
Wendy Wright
EDITORS Barbara Delissen, Luna Soo,
Branislava Vladisavljevic
IMAGE RESEARCHERS
Kylie McLaughlin, Aude Vauconsant
PRE-PRESS PRODUCTION Ryan Evans
PRINT PRODUCTION Larissa Frost

WRITTEN BY Ann Abel, Johanna Ashby, Brett
Atkinson, Alexis Averbuck, Sarah Baxter, Oliver
Bennett, Sarah Bennett, Joe Bindloss, Abigail
Blasi, Claire Boobbyer, Stuart Butler, Jean-Bernard
Carillet , Lucy Corne, Chris Deliso, Sam Haddad,
Tom Hall, Damian Harper, Tienlon Ho, Trent Holden,
Catherine Le Nevez, Nana Luckham, Anirban
Mahapatra, Emily Matchar, Craig McLachlan,
John Noble, Becky Ohlsen, Lorna Parkes, Brandon
Presser, Kevin Raub, Simon Richmond, Dan Savery
Raz, Tamara Sheward, Benedict Walker, Luke
Waterson, Chris Zeiher, Karla Zimmerman

THANKS TO Larissa Frost, Chris Girdler,
Jane Hart, Annelies Mertens, Florian Poppe,
Wibowo Rusli, Tracy Whitmey

**Best in Travel starts with hundreds of ideas from
everyone at Lonely Planet, including our extended family
of travellers, bloggers and tweeters. Once we're confident
we have the cream of 2014's travel choices, the final
selection is made by a panel of in-house travel experts,
based on topicality, excitement, value and that special
X-factor. Our focus is on the merits of each destination
and the unique experiences they offer travellers.**

October 2013
ISBN 978 1 74321 728 3
Published by Lonely Planet Publications Pty Ltd
ABN 36 005 607 983
90 Maribyrnong St, Footscray,
Victoria, 3011, Australia
www.lonelyplanet.com

Printed in China
10 9 8 7 6 5 4 3 2 1
© Lonely Planet 2013
© Photographers as indicated 2013

LONELY PLANET OFFICES

Australia Locked Bag 1, Footscray, Victoria, 3011
Phone 03 8379 8000
Email talk2us@lonelyplanet.com.au

USA 150 Linden St, Oakland, CA 94607
Phone 510 250 6400 Toll free 800 275 8555
Email info@lonelyplanet.com

UK Media Centre, 201 Wood Lane, London W12 7TQ
Phone 020 8433 1333
Email go@lonelyplanet.co.uk

Although the authors and Lonely Planet have taken all
reasonable care in preparing this book, we make no warranty
about the accuracy or completeness of its content and, to the
maximum extent permitted, disclaim all liability from its use.

Front Cover Image African elephants - Steve Bloom/Getty Images

MIX
Paper from
responsible sources
FSC™ C021741

Paper in this book is certified against
the Forest Stewardship Council™
standards. FSC™ promotes
environmentally responsible, socially
beneficial and economically viable
management of the world's forests.

TRAVEL PLANNER

LONELY PLANET'S BEST IN TRAVEL 2014

JANUARY

500th Anniversary of the Foundation of Trinidad, Cuba The anniversary of the city's foundation by Spanish conquistadors is celebrated with a variety of fiestas and cultural events.

WinterPRIDE: Gay & Lesbian Ski Week, Canada Guys and gals from far and wide descend upon Whistler's slopes for a week of snowy antics and ski-instructor impersonators from 26 January to 2 February.

Chinese New Year, China On 31 January 2014, the Chinese New Year welcomes in the year of the horse. People born in the year of the horse are active, extrovert, sexy and vivacious: it promises to be a vintage Shanghai year.

FEBRUARY

Coast to Coast, New Zealand Real athletes run-cycle-kayak the world-famous West Coast epic 243km to Christchurch from near Kumara, a normally quiet coast town that turns into Piccadilly Circus on 14 and 15 February.

Carnaval, Brazil Some two million revellers converge amid sun, sand and samba during Rio de Janeiro's annual Carnaval celebrations from 28 February to 4 March.

Losar, India Masked Buddhist deities and infernal demons come to life in full sartorial splendour during vibrant chaam dances that take place across Sikkim in the February or March run-up to Tibetan New Year.